D0149498

Praise for *Negotiating Success*

"Jim Hornickel has crafted a book that requires fearless self-examination and a willingness to change how you operate. This book is filled with practical tools for professionals who seek to be more effective in a matrix structure. He doesn't attempt to assert conflict avoidance; rather, he constructs an open and systematic program to reduce the opportunity for misunderstandings and win-lose scenarios.

"Hornickel provides a straightforward approach to developing a comprehensive method to effectively communicate via a personal code of conduct and sharing that code with your collaborators. I'd recommend this for anyone who works in an environment that requires negotiations."

—Dietrich Thompson, HR Manager, Microsoft Corporation

"Negotiating Success is an inspiring book whose time has come. While hard skills are critical in negotiations, soft skills make up the essential ingredients that support mutually agreeable gains. Jim's blend of the two shows how to make the negotiating process human again. His approach on supporting the other in getting what they want invokes reciprocal behavior. This book shows that conflict is not inevitable for sessions to be successful. The reader will raise his/her emotional intelligence, learn the principles of ethical influence, and still come away with the skills and steps to negotiate intelligently. Hard skills with soft edges; that's the winning formula!"

—Michael Connor
Bridge Partnership, author of *Insights of a Father*,
www.insightsofafather.com

"In addition to being right on target with teaching and polishing negotiating skills, this is a page-turner! Leave it to you, Jim, to create a great teaching manual and an enjoyable read! Nicely done, my friend."

—Jeff Eisensmith, Department of Homeland Security,
Chief Information Security Officer

"This book is exhaustive, concise, simple, and accessible to everyone. You find all you need to know to master negotiation, techniques, processes, and examples.

"The knowledge shared with the reader is useful and applicable in many situations or moments we face in life. I would recommend it not only to a sales person or project manager newly appointed, but also to students and young adults starting in life, parents, and teenagers.

"This approach gives equal importance; first to the people, and second to the techniques engaged in the negotiation process. The whole negotiation is seen as a successful relationship between individuals and not a game you must win."

—Laurent Belle-Perat, Schneider Electric, Global Marketing,
Saudi Arabia; Internal Marketing and
Communications Manager, Middle East

"Jim Hornickel is a master at negotiations and relationship building. Throughout this thoughtful book on negotiation skills, Jim brings sensitivity to the negotiating relationship so that all parties feel honored and well-satisfied with the outcomes. Jim has shared his negotiation insights in a way that adds real depth and fulfillment to the myriad of interactions we have each day at work, home, and play."
—Suzanne Guthrie, editor of *Managing From The Inside Out*

"*Negotiating Success* is not just another book on negotiation, but instead presents a unique and brave approach to win-win from a genuine and human perspective rather than a clichéd one. It concisely presents the best in negotiation research and techniques and offers practical advice that will inspire negotiators in any situation to live up to the highest standards of their profession.

"Going beyond commonplace, overly simplistic and counterproductive tactics, it provides an innovative and thoughtful alternative. In an overcrowded category, *Negotiating Success* differentiates itself by challenging the reader to take a holistic and elevated approach to negotiation with skills, techniques, and personal development that works!"
—Vito Loconte, VP, Global Client Finance,
United Kingdom IPG Mediabrands

"Negotiation is something that occurs on a daily basis—from a small conversation regarding a work task completion to a more complex agreement on contractual KPI's. Having a resource that can offer a guide for the interacting process that dissolves conflict and builds rapport is so important. This book serves this purpose in a clear and comprehensive manner, effectively contributing to working relationships that facilitate the necessary pace of today's working world."
—Sarah Sexton, HR Manager,
MWH Global, Doha, Qatar

"The fortunate ones who read Jim's work will have an epiphany. The suggestion that all human interaction involves negotiating is profound. Focus outside of the workplace and realize the broad application his book provides. It can facilitate beneficial dialogue between spouses, children, neighbors, and practically everyone with whom we come in contact.

"Additionally, leading with mutuality and respect will result in more simple negotiations, stronger relationships, and a rewarding career . . . a must read!"
—Robert Torsey, Management Consultant
(Former VP at ALCOA)

"Negotiations are sometimes seen as (hard) games, with a winner and a loser. With this book, Jim brings back the humanity in negotiations. If you want to bring your negotiation skills to the next level or . . . see negotiations from a whole different perspective, you should read this book! It not only gives you thorough background information, but it also gives you very practical 'next steps' that will take you through the process."
—Gabby Staal, President & Founder of LeaderQuest,
Partners in Evolution, The Netherlands

"Jim Hornickel delivers the essential keys to successful negotiations: combining the hard skills with the soft edges that create constructive outcomes for all parties.

"Embrace the tools and principles of *Negotiating Success* so you're fully prepared in advance of all your meaningful negotiations. Learn to stay true to your values, foresee others' needs, motives and desired results, and move confidently through any discomfort and uncertainty on the path to establishing a win-win.

"It's all here, structured flexibly so you can organize and leverage the tools that best suit your background, situation, and intentions. Enjoy the process—and make the world a better place while you're at it."

—Ken Jacobsen, President, CourageWorks, Inc.

"Jim Hornickel has drawn from such diverse disciplines as neurology, psychology, and physiology to deliver a transformative book which is conversational and interactive. Scenarios, examples, and templates allow the user to holistically integrate the concepts. Thought provoking questions for self-inquiry go beyond just teaching theory to facilitating inner shifts in awareness. This prepares the reader for skilled negotiation by starting with self-knowledge and moving to understanding human nature. From Hornickel's vast experience in the field he provides clear, solid, proven approaches. Anyone involved in conflict resolution, whether in relationships, business, or diplomatic communication, will benefit from reading this."

—Susan Lynne
Management Consultant
Susan Lynne Development, Toronto

"Every once in a while, a truly insightful and practical guide makes its way to our collective hands and hearts—this is the case with Hornickel's latest book, *Negotiating Success*. At a time when so many work cultures are embedded in fierce competition and an emphasis on individual success, this publication provides a thoughtful, respectful, and alternative approach to negotiating 'what you want.' A highly respected and successful leader, Hornickel convincingly espouses a win-win perspective as key to achieving mutually successful and satisfying negotiations. This is a book that I will refer to time and time again."

—Jan Janssen, Manager, Upper Tier Municipal Government,
and author of human interest
articles about community, self-care, women,
values, consciousness, etc., Ontario, Canada

"When emotions are high, intelligence is low. *Negotiating Success* creates an eye-opening journey about how we can develop interactions with others using our greater consciousness to get what we want when the stakes are high.

"*Negotiating Success* is a must read for anyone looking to improve their personal and professional power in effective communications at a deeper level."

—Loretta Peters, Personal Brand and
Online Identity Strategist,
www.EnterprisingCareers.com

"*Negotiating Success* is a must read for anyone who has acknowledged the benefits of win-win negotiating, but has struggled executing at the table. In simple, direct, and actionable language, Jim breaks down the challenges we all face in taking on new habits or behaviors.

"Jim shares the how and why behind breaking negotiating habits that don't serve you and learning new ones that lead to a more effective outcome and a better business relationship. Having worked with Jim on many occasions, take my word for it and buy this book. Read this book, and then put the message of this book into action!"

—Dan Demers, President, ReMission Consulting, Inc.
www.ReMissionConsulting.com

"CEO's will find *Negotiating Success* a detailed handbook for developing win-win negotiating skills within their team. The book is useful as an introduction to the subject, but its real value is as a manual to lead a process of continuing to improve the team's negotiating and customer relationships skills. Mr. Hornickel writes in a very conversational tone, mixing advice with real life case studies to develop win-win negotiating skills within your team."

—Matthew Falls, Partner, Growthers

"*Negotiating Success* answers the question which every human being asks: How can I get what I want out of life without the unexpected and unwanted repercussions and, at the same time, generate and maintain real happiness for myself and others?

"Jim Hornickel's template is the very thing you need to accomplish that which secretly drives you and every other human being on this planet.

"Don't read this book. Eat and savor it. Take time to digest it. In doing so, you will walk into a new you and a new future. A future that you and everyone else will appreciate and wish to duplicate."

—Barry Curtis, Barry Curtis and Associates

"Haven't most of us taken the time to build a reference library, whether it has to do with health, cooking, home repairs, investing, and probably a few on relationships? Well, along comes another must-have to add to your collection—*Negotiating Success*—which after you note the subtitle you understand that it will apply to situations you encounter every day professionally, personally, and otherwise. The bonus is that *Negotiating Success* is much more than a reference book. It is really a how-to manual which offers in-depth understanding on how agreements are formed, compromises developed, and goals attained, as well as a personal development guide to help us in our daily activities involving human interaction. Jim Hornickel has left no stone unturned. What a valuable book he has delivered."

—Joe Harding, Assistant Women's Basketball Coach,
Flagler College

Negotiating Success

Success

TIPS AND TOOLS FOR **BUILDING RAPPORT** AND **DISSOLVING CONFLICT** WHILE STILL **GETTING WHAT YOU WANT**

JIM HORNICKEL

WILEY

Published by John Wiley & Sons, Inc., Hoboken, New Jersey.

Published simultaneously in Canada.

For general information about our other products and services, please contact our Customer Care Department within the United States at (800) 762-2974, outside the United States at (317) 572-3993 or fax (317) 572-4002.

Wiley publishes in a variety of print and electronic formats and by print-on-demand. Some material included with standard print versions of this book may not be included in e-books or in print-on-demand. If this book refers to media such as a CD or DVD that is not included in the version you purchased, you may download this material at http://booksupport.wiley.com. For more information about Wiley products, visit www.wiley.com.

Library of Congress Cataloging-in-Publication Data:

Hornickel, Jim, 1952-
  Negotiating success: tips and tools for building rapport and dissolving conflict while still getting what you want/Jim Hornickel.
    pages cm
  Includes index.
  ISBN 978-1-118-68871-7 (hardback); ISBN 978-1-118-83693-4 (ebk); ISBN 978-1-118-83702-3 (ebk)
  1. Negotiation in business. 2. Negotiation. 3. Conflict management. 4. Emotional intelligence. I. Title.
    HD58.6.H67 2014
    158'.5–dc23

                                                                    2013034340

Printed in the United States of America

10 9 8 7 6 5 4 3 2 1

Contents

Introduction

All conversations are negotiations. Whether small personal exchanges or large, complex business contracts, we are negotiating all the time. Two key questions are: "What negotiating skills do you have to work with?" and "Who are you being as you negotiate?"

Negotiation skills have been around since Neanderthals determined who would go out and fight the saber-toothed tiger. What has been added in these recent, more enlightened times is attention to negotiation relationships.

You are now embarking on the exciting next steps in negotiating mastery to become ever more aware of using "mutuality" as the way forward. You are at the launch point for taking bold new directions on how to model, teach, and inspire mutual satisfaction in negotiations.

When negotiations are built on the goal of having both sides win, magic happens. Individual and company values are met, visions are achieved, and the organization's needs are fulfilled in the short term and over time. Even in a world that values competition so strongly, when you go for win-win, *you* will be at the leading edge of this change.

Negotiating involves "hard skills"—steps, phases, and strategies; but it also requires "soft skills"—building positive and productive relationships. We address both major areas in this work.

These pages are designed for you to come back to as often as you require for review. The material in this book is intended to help you grow your mastery over the next days, weeks, months, and years. Yours will be a journey of discovery, practice, and integration. Each chapter ends with a series of questions to probe. I suggest that you write/type each answer. Then use the S.M.A.R.T. goal-setting formula shown to make your next steps toward mastery concrete.

I am honored to be a part of your dynamic growth and fulfillment!

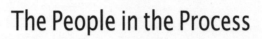

The People in the Process

1

Valuing Mutuality, Proactivity, and R.E.S.P.E.C.T.

The *Negotiating Success* model is based on three equally important principles: Mutuality, Proactivity, and R.E.S.P.E.C.T.
(see Figure 1.1). Together they form the cornerstones of the
negotiating process.

Mutuality

People around the world have been deeply indoctrinated in the
concept of win-lose. Although that may produce some excitement
for a sports event, or create drama in elections, it is simply

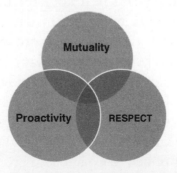

FIGURE 1.1   The Cornerstones of the Negotiating Process

self-defeating in negotiations. The best results in the short and long run will be to work on behalf of each party getting as much of what is wanted as possible.

Changing from win-lose to mutuality, or win-win, takes a mental paradigm shift. And change is not easy, but change will come more quickly if you have an incentive. The motivation to become a mutuality-based negotiator is in part the self-serving factor. You do need to win on "your" side. But so does the other party. So why stop with only half of the equation served? What do you imagine life would be like if we all changed from *self-serving only* to *self-serving while serving others*? Life is full of choices and this is one of them. And it makes total sense.

The principle of reciprocity (more in Chapter 5) says that when we serve others, they will most likely be inclined to return the favor. You do not need to "believe" this. Check it out in your own life. If someone has no interest in helping you, are you more or less likely to help them? But if someone acts in ways that support and serve your cause, are you more or less inclined to help and support that person? If this is true for you, it is likely true for the other, too.

Like so many of the ideas in this book, mutuality will be stronger in formal negotiations if you practice win-win interactions regularly, everywhere. Here is where the self-serving factor comes into play again. Although mutuality-based negotiations work for everyone in the short and long term, there is also a personal W.I.I.F.M. (What's In It For Me) involved. What is in it for you to practice more mutuality in day-to-day life? Here is where science and the ancient masters are in agreement.

Perhaps, like me, your academic days are a few years back. What we learned could only be what was known at the time. If you were a classmate of Columbus, you would have been taught, and probably believed, that the world was flat. Inconceivable now that we so clearly know that is not true. Well, the science of biology has also continued to expand and grow. New technologic advances are forever showing us new information. That new information shows how old "knowledge" and "beliefs" need to be updated. One area of the new biology (circa 1995) is about genome expression: epigenetics. What does this have to do with negotiations? We are talking about the satisfaction involved in mutuality.

Here is how it works. Science (via the Swiss physician Friedrich Miescher) had its first rudimentary identification of DNA in 1869 (it was always there, but like many things, we simply could not see it). Then we could not understand it. Then we have what we think is the understanding. Then that understanding changes. In the mid-1990s, Dr. Bruce Lipton and others, with the help of ever-advancing technology, found a major difference about DNA. It was said that DNA is the blueprint of life. It was thought to determine lots of who we are and what we do. But the new science observed that while DNA is indeed a blueprint, it is influenced to direct us by energies outside of itself. Simply put, when DNA received signals that are negative (whether from within us or from our external environment), the DNA expresses negatively. When positive signals reach the DNA, it expresses positively.

Let's take this back to mutuality and personal satisfaction. Studies show this: When people perform acts of service or kindness (the start in mutuality), our DNA likes that and expresses it in ways that feel good to us. Personal satisfaction! The studies also reveal that the person receiving the act of service or perceived kindness also feels good. And happily, even people who only observe acts of service also feel just about as good as the giver and receiver. All influenced by positive genome expression.

Take these human factors into the negotiation sessions. When making offers and trading concessions with positive giving and receiving, the process feels better. The outcomes are more rewarding to both parties. The memory of that serves well in future negotiations. If you doubt that, remember how you felt and what thoughts you had when you were bargaining with people who only had their own self-interest in mind. Did their methods inspire you? Probably the opposite. For most of us, when we feel pushed too hard by someone who is out to get concessions from us but not give back in return, we go to acting the same way. That becomes win-lose. In the long run, win-lose is really lose-lose. You are bound to go into next negotiations with a jaundiced eye and ready for combat instead of intelligent exchanges.

To finish this small look at mutuality, it remains true that there will always be some professionals who are so deeply programmed in win-lose that you simply will not inspire them to change. You will be forced to do what you need to do to get what you and your organization wants. That is reality. But life is all about doing what you can, when you can, with whom you can. Let us take that into the next section on proactivity.

Proactivity

Because of the deeply entrenched win-lose training we have talked about, the ball will often be in your court to lead the way to mutuality-based negotiating. What an amazing opportunity each one of us has to influence positive change. And again, the beauty of this positive change is that *everyone* wins.

Start the shift now. Begin with yourself. Reflect on your competitive attitudes and actions. Do they serve you as effectively as a win-win approach would? Try little experiments of asking for what you want while seeing how you can help others get what they want, too.

For example, a parent has been in the habit with his or her child of often saying no. Mom has been working at her demanding job all day and when she gets home, she just wants to kick back for a while and read the newspaper. Son Mike says to her, "Mommy, would you play cards with me?" Instead of an immediate no, consider that Mike might simply need some of your time and attention. Playing cards is just one strategy that could get him that. In a mutuality-based interaction, you might ask Mike to get up on your lap and read some of the newspaper to him. That could be win-win. Creativity is a key component of finding mutual routes to satisfaction. We return to expanding creativity later in this book.

Remember, it will most likely be you who has to lead the way to learning that there are more rewarding ways of negotiating than the ingrained competitive, win-lose approach.

R.E.S.P.E.C.T

By now you might accept that mutuality-based negotiations are good for everyone. You might also be musing on how you can be more of a leader in proactively infusing the negotiations process with win-win attitudes and actions. We now take a look at how the qualities and practices of R.E.S.P.E.C.T. will add to the positive possibilities. We take a peek into how respect-laden negotiations will serve you and the party you are trading with.

R. esponsiveness

What is responsiveness? The dictionary definitions include: answering and replying, reacting to suggestions, influences, appeals and efforts. Negotiations entail a series of exchanges. More specifically, they involve exchanges of information, ideas, suggestions, requests, and concessions. The more the communication is one-sided during the process, the weaker one side feels: disempowered. That party will be less motivated to share critical information. And withdrawal or withholding imposes unhelpful limits. Less information with reduced cooperation does not serve either side!

Increasing responsiveness then is a mutually beneficial attitude and practice in negotiations. Starting in the Discovery Phase (Chapter 12), make it clear that you intend on being responsive to their needs and that you expect them to be responsive to yours.

Reciprocity! Clearly get their agreement and do not proceed until you do so. If you are responding to their arguments but they are not responding to yours, stop the process and remind them that you both agreed to responsiveness as an integral part of negotiating.

For example, let us say that you have been in a fairly good flow of information exchange and, at some point, the other party puts a brake on the flow. If you are consciously, actively aware of the responsiveness factor, you know to stop the negotiation and explore the new gap. What has occurred to change the other party's cooperation? What possible pressures have arisen for them? Are they using a tactic? (More to come in Chapter 16.) Paying attention to responsiveness will only serve to help moving forward or regain the flow of mutually beneficial exchange.

E. mpathy

What is empathy? Various dictionary definitions include: the ability and willingness to understand and relate to the feelings of another. Both sides will come into a bargaining session with worries, unmet goals, personal pressures, and needs. That is just the way it is. Empathy is the willingness and ability to put yourself in their shoes as best you can. You must intellectually understand their problems and, more critically, *feel* their pain.

Why is emotional connection to someone else's pain important? Most behavior styles appreciate when someone outside themselves can relate. They do not feel so alone. In mutuality-based negotiating, the whole idea is to constantly relate to the other party's need throughout the negotiating process (even as you take care of your own needs). And one area of needs will be emotional, even if it is not openly spoken about (more on emotional intelligence in Chapter 3).

Let us stress that empathizing is not agreeing; it is simply acknowledging something that is truly going on for the other person.

Also remember that the old demand to "leave your emotions at the door" is pretty much impossible for human beings. We can manage to the best of our ability, but part of our very biological structure is to have emotions. Our brains have a thought and then our brain sends a chemical message to our body saying "this thought equals this emotion."

Think of a time in your life when you were especially troubled by some event or circumstance. It does not matter whether it was at work or home. And pick an instance when someone around you let you know that they could relate to what you were going through; that they cared about you. Most of us appreciate that. Most people feel supported by what the person did or said. That feeling of support creates a certain level of bonding. And negotiations simply go better when the participants feel more rather than less connection with the other. In mediation, a form of negotiation, the first thing done is to find common ground. Empathy helps establish common ground.

Please, do not believe or disbelieve this but check it out in the relationships in your own life.

So, the unmet goals, pressures, needs, and so on, will be part of just about any negotiation. And that predictability will serve you. Anticipate that you will have ample opportunities to empathize with their situation(s). Find ways to relate via empathy. This common ground will absolutely enhance the relationship between or among you.

Here is one last suggestion: Tailor your empathy to the style of the other party, using your knowledge of their negotiation style (from Chapter 4). Everyone processes differently, and one style of empathizing will not be right for all personality types. To be effective, you have to meet people where they are.

S. ervice

Mutuality-based negotiating means *being of service to each other*. Think of customer service. What are all of the personal traits and effective behaviors that make a good customer service interaction for you? Do you appreciate when someone is attentive and responsive to your needs? Treats you like you want to be treated? Has a "Can Do!" attitude and set of actions? How pleased are you when someone serves you? How displeased are you when you get poor service?

The same effects of providing good or poor service are part and parcel of the negotiation process. Imagine these approaches being used with you from the other party: respectfulness, honor, truthfulness, caring, positive attitude, honesty. Imagine actions that include: deep listening, quick and thorough responses, organized interchanges. These approaches and actions are all aspects of good service—negotiations thrive when they are present.

An example: You have done your preparation (Chapter 11) for a negotiation session. You know what you can and cannot offer. You start the conversation in the discovery phase by designing an agreement that states that each of you will work with the other (to be of service) to have a good enough, win-win outcome. The other side asks for a concession. Again, you know what you can and cannot give. In a strong but empathetic voice, you say, "Well, we can't give you that, but here is what we *can* give you." If what you offer is needed by the other side, there will be a feeling of service connected with the exchange. Constantly look for ways to serve the people and the process.

P. erspectives

What is a perspective? It is frequently defined as a point of view, belief, or opinion.

When two or more parties come together in the negotiation process, there are likely to be at least two or more perspectives to deal with. In fact, every aspect of a negotiation will have its own set of perspectives riding along.

When do perspectives derail the proceedings? When people get positional. When they are entrenched in a perspective and it is the only perspective or view they can see (or care to see). Movement bogs down when only one perspective is active.

When do perspectives enhance the proceedings? When people consciously look for as many perspectives as possible. When parties pool these perspectives and then look to see which one or ones will be most effective for both sides winning.

Most of us have never had a course in finding the right perspectives. Standard academia simply does not address this vital process. So, most people do not know that they are the ones who choose their point of view in every moment of life. It just takes a new radar screen, a new intention of perspective-awareness to start finding the truth of this.

Here is an exercise to play with to deepen your understanding of perspectives and ability to choose yours at will. Think of a current, somewhat negative situation in your life (personal or professional) that is unresolved. For an example, we use the tough situation of being told you have a form of cancer (not life-threatening at this point). Did you know you have a choice in how you respond? The following methodology will make it clearer.

For the sake of keeping the process simple here, we look at only two contrasting perspectives: "This Is Hard" and "I Can Handle This." (In real life, there are unlimited points of view to choose from—more to come in Chapter 8 and creativity.) We just name the situation *Cancer* and first look at it through the eyes of the more negative perspective, This Is Hard.

Thoughts: From the perspective of This Is Hard, what thoughts will you have? Some might include: "Why me?" "How will my family take this bad news?" "Who will pay for all of the medical co-pays?" "I'll never be able to sleep at night worrying about what will happen." And so on.

Emotions: Thoughts produce emotions within us. The emotions you might have when strongly in the perspective of

This Is Hard might be: "I feel—anger, sadness, fear, confusion, and so on."

Body sensations: Thoughts produce chemicals that are sent throughout the body; we call them emotions. These chemicals also produce body sensations that can be felt and observed. If you are angry, you might have a tensed jaw. Sadness might be felt in your eyes. Fear could show up as a knot in your stomach. Confusion may be felt as an uneasy feeling all over.

Summary: All of these thoughts, emotions, and body sensations are responses to the way we look at something: in this case, the situation of cancer as viewed through the lens of This Is Hard.

Now let's put that point of view aside and try on another. The situation of cancer remains exactly the same, but this time you try on looking at it through the lens of I Can Handle This.

Thoughts: "Even though this is a surprise, I've had lots of surprises in life. I can take this one on." "I can beat this!" "This is important and I'll find a way to pay for the medical expenses." "I realize even more so how precious life is." "Millions of people have survived cancer; I will, too!" "Because of this wake-up call, I will celebrate more of my successes." And so on.

Emotions: "I feel hopeful, strong, determined, and so on."

Body sensations: The chemicals of emotion that your new thoughts produce might be felt in your body as powerful hands, lighter all around, resolute facial muscles, and so on.

Summary: These thoughts, feelings, and body sensations will be different from the first example. Which set do you think will serve you and others in your circle in a more positive way: the first or second?

The idea is to become aware that each of us is in charge of how we view life and its circumstances. And that also includes the point(s) of view we take during negotiations. It is good to notice when the frame of mind we are in is moving the process forward or setting up roadblocks. We have the capacity to shift how we are looking at anything. And although we do not directly control how the other party views the bargaining, we can influence how they look. Asking powerful questions (to come later), pointing out information or possibilities missed, increasing creativity . . . all can add to the number of options we have in looking at any and all things.

It takes willingness to look for effective perspectives. It also takes skill to invite them out so that both parties can peacefully select those perspectives best serving the end goal of mutual gain.

E. steem

Esteem is the state of one's self-worth. People can have low self-esteem, high self-esteem, or be anywhere in between.

Why pay attention to your own and others' self-esteem in negotiations? Low self-esteem will produce fear and uncertainty, which are qualities that do not lend themselves to vibrant, positive trading. High-esteem sets the stage for uplifting interactions, so both parties are involved here.

You: What do you need to do to keep your own self-esteem at its highest levels? Part of this is how you look at yourself throughout life—a subject larger than this book deals with. But true nonetheless. There are things that you can do in negotiations to bolster your sense of self-worth.

One way to feel good about yourself is to make sure that you stay true to your values. Negotiations can get tricky. They can also get dirty. If you lose sight of mutuality (if a value of yours is that everyone can get a good enough outcome), then you may find yourself playing the win-lose game that others may practice. Your self-esteem may slip by doing that.

Another positive step you can take is to be as prepared as time and available information allows. Have you ever been caught short, knowing that you really could have done a better job beforehand? You might have played the blame game—blaming yourself or others or circumstances. None of that raises esteem. Doing what you have committed to do and doing it as well as possible goes a long way to having you feel okay about your efforts and about yourself (better esteem).

Other: Although the other negotiating party is ultimately responsible for their own self-esteem (as we all are), we do have influence on how they feel. Looking for opportunities to empathize or serve will bring more positive results to negotiating. A practice of raising self-esteem in others is also a positive option. We call it "Catching People Doing Something Right." There are three useful methodologies for catching people doing something right:

1. *Praise:* This is a general positive comment that is intended to have the other person feeling good. In a negotiation it could sound something like: "Thanks for pointing it out that way." There is no real substance to the communication you just offered, but the tone of it is uplifting.

2. *Acknowledgment:* This is positive feedback filled with more specifics. You might say: "Thank you for telling me that my offer was a bit off track. You stated what was true but your tone of voice was not judgmental and you seemed to understand that I made an honest mistake."

3. *Appreciation:* This last method of more esteem-raising feedback is probably the least commonly used but goes to the next level. *Praise* is general, *acknowledgment* is specific, and *appreciation* speaks to the underlying qualities or character traits that fuel what you are praising or appreciating. Not everyone deals with life on this level. But if you are someone who does, and if your negotiating partner does, too, it is very enriching. To end with the example we have been using, you might say something like: "Thank you for your honesty in

telling me that. I think that took *courage*. It also took some *caring* on your part to do your best to not have me feel foolish for my obvious mistake."

In summary, notice your impact on others. Do you act in ways that put down the other party? Do you stomp on their values during negotiations? Or, do you look for every available opportunity to raise the other's spirits and to champion the other's efforts? It is a no-brainer that negotiations that promote high self-esteem on both sides will produce more welcome results on both personal and business levels.

C. ourage

Courage here means the ability to move through discomfort and uncertainty on behalf of a win-win negotiation.

Negotiations are filled with emotions. Pressures abound. Differing personal styles create degrees of comfort and discomfort. Most negotiators do not consciously check in on their feelings. There is a real drawback to pushing aside the emotions that are not only real within us but are also messengers (more to come on emotional intelligence in Chapter 3).

What is the connection between feelings and courage? You would not need courage if you were not afraid or apprehensive or cautious. These emotions, and others, can and do hold people back. If you are like most of us, they sometimes hold you back, too. If you were not raised in a family that dealt openly with emotions or have not taken it on yourself to consciously attend to your emotions, you may have an internal learning curve on this subject. But it is well worth it (again, more to come later).

Courage, then, is the ability, by degree, to face uncomfortable feelings. There are negotiators who use intimidation. They want to overpower you to get what they want. They are not win-win players. There are many reasons for their being that way, but what you get to deal with is how they are in your negotiation sessions.

So stepping through the discomfort takes courage. Why would you do that? Because there is a lot at stake professionally and personally. Professionally, you have your success on the line in each and every negotiation. Personally, you have your values and self-worth (self-esteem) at risk.

For example, you are negotiating for a car with a bully salesperson. While it is always a choice to walk away, even that can take courage for some people. So you are in a discussion where it feels like the dealership is getting all of the benefits. Every time you request a possible concession they can give, perhaps upgrading the stereo system if you finance with them, they have an argument that denies you. You could cave in from the pressure to stop asking for what you want (because that is what it really is). Or you could bring the conversation to a halt, stand firm in posture, tone, and attitude, and explain why there will be no sale if they do not cooperate in trading. But to do that, you may well have to overcome the negative voices within you. You will probably have to acknowledge the knot in your stomach (fear) and say what you need to say in spite of old habits of backing down. All of that takes an inner strength and commitment from what we call *courage*.

Like everything else in life, increasing your courage will not simply happen on the spot in heated negotiations because you want it to. Increasing courage takes time and practice. It really needs to become a way of life. When you incrementally increase your ability to face your fears (large and small) on a daily basis, you will absolutely be stronger in times of greater challenge, like during intense negotiations.

"How do I increase my courage?" you ask. Again, this is a process that takes time, but you have to start somewhere. Start small—very small is fine. Take a moment to identify something that repeatedly causes you to feel a little uncomfortable—something that has held you back from asking for what you want or doing what you want. Examples are everywhere for most of us.

For instance, you might want to tell a best friend or partner something that has not set well with you for some time. What would make it a little easier for you to broach the subject? Think about what would be in it for them (W.I.I.F.M.) to do something about it. What tone of voice might you use in addressing your issue? How might you empathize with how they view things? Plan a strategy in advance as to what you will say and how you will say it. Have a plan for what you will do or say if they do not receive your comment or suggestion well. Step into your courage and give it a try.

After you have survived that (and you will), make it a practice—once a day works well—to do something a little courageous. Like any other muscle, the courage muscle needs exercise to be strong when it really counts.

And it really counts in negotiations. It certainly takes courage to lead the way to mutuality, when others do not know the way. They may actively buck the way. It can take courage to make requests for what you really want. But negotiations are typically a series of requests and responses. It takes courage to stand up for your personal values in the heat of some bargaining sessions. It takes courage to face conflict head on. But again, the more you practice anywhere, the more courage you will have everywhere.

T. ruth-Telling

Truth-telling goes hand in hand with courage. Telling the truth can be defined as the avoidance of lying, deception, misrepresentation, and nondisclosure.

We start with lying. Let's define lying as an *intentional* misrepresentation of an objective truth. What happens in any relationship (and negotiators are in a bargaining relationship) when one person knowingly lies to the other? When the truth becomes known, when the act of lying is revealed, mistrust follows. Mistrust in a negotiation will inevitably turn it into a contest of wariness—win-lose if you will.

Even though we cover tactics in Chapter 16, an initial conversation fits in perfectly here. For the sake of this mutuality-based negotiations book, a *strategy* is defined as a plan of action designed to achieve a goal. A *tactic* is a purposeful set of actions designed to put you in a weaker position. There is quite a difference in intent and often in outcome between the two.

Let's come back to lying and the byproduct, mistrust, by using an example of a tactic. Let's say that you are negotiating while selling your car to a relative. Like a good negotiator, and even though they are kin, you spent a little time getting to know the potential buyer a bit better. You found more common ground and feel an even stronger degree of trust with your young cousin. You have also established your range and alternatives (more to come in Chapter 9). You know what your bottom line is: in this case, the least you will take for the car before walking away from the negotiation. You feel like you are at least in the general ballpark but you know you need to get more than is being offered. Then your relative uses the tactic "Empty Pockets." When still too far apart for a sale, he tells you the last figure offered is all he has; that is the absolute limit. You are torn because you need the money as a down payment for your next car, but after all, this is family. So against your inner voice of better judgment, you sign the title over to him despite being short the money you wanted from the transaction. Later, you find out from this cousin's older sister that their father basically told his son, your cousin, that he would fund the car with an amount quite a bit higher than your cousin admitted to. You were deceived! You were lied to! How does that make you feel? Disappointed? Angry? Resentful? These are not emotions that will have you wanting to see that cousin anytime soon.

The same set of dynamics occurs time and again in transactional or win-lose business negotiations. For a short-term gain, people lie or misrepresent and the result is always going to be future mistrust. If you were the liar, and if this is truly a one-time-only negotiation, you will not have to deal with the losing person's distrusting attitude again. Okay, the deception won't come back to bite you from out there. But you will still have to live with yourself. Your integrity and authenticity have been compromised. Although you may have gotten the physical gain, you are losing on the ethical plane.

But the process of negotiating is not a simple one. We can't kid ourselves; negotiating is a dance of revealing and not revealing. A good negotiator never puts everything on the table unless the relationship is deeply established; a tried and true history of trust. But there is a major difference between intelligently encouraging discovery of what the other has and will give and trying to take him or her for all they are worth via lying.

Still, it is hard for many of us to be as truthful as would serve a mutuality-based process. Many of us have been trained from an early age to lie to protect ourselves, to cover our butts. Or at least not tell the whole truth. Our training starts with not wanting to get "in trouble" with our parents and teachers and continues on to our relationships with our boss. Every layer of holdback weakens trust and diminishes possibilities. If disclosure equals trust and we are afraid to tell the truth (to disclose), the process stumbles and bumbles along.

Truth-telling is even more powerful when it is compassionate. Empathy again comes into play. Look ahead to see what the impact might be on the other person from your truth-telling. This is not a license to blast people with your truth. Remember, whatever you have to say is only your perspective. So tell the truth as you see it with some wiggle room for others to have a different reality. Then try to meet somewhere in the middle.

Mutuality, Proactivity, and R.E.S.P.E.C.T. Summary

You are a powerful force for the good when you negotiate with mutuality at the center of the process, when you lead the way proactively and with positivity, and when everything you do is done with R.E.S.P.E.C.T.

Questions to Ponder

- What has been your training regarding win-lose?
- What has been your experience of win-win?
- What would be in it for you (W.I.I.F.M.) to be more mutuality-based?
- How reactive are you in your day-to-day life?
- How proactive are you?
- What are your leadership strengths and weaknesses?
- What is your current degree of responsiveness?
- How empathetic have you been of late?
- Are you willing to look for five opportunities a day to empathize?
- What is your attitude about being of service; everywhere?
- How will you find ways to be of service more often?
- What can you do to improve your awareness about perspectives?
- At any given moment, what perspective are you in?
- How is that perspective serving you?
- What do you need to do to find a better point of view to act from?
- What is your general current level of self-esteem?
- What can you do to bolster your own esteem?
- Are you willing to look for opportunities to raise self-esteem in others?
- On a scale of 1 to 10, what is your current overall level of courage?
- What kinds of things provoke fear or discomfort in you?
- What will you do to confront your fears more regularly?
- What is your current degree of truth-telling?
- What happens within you and in the outside world when you lie?
- How does it feel when you tell the truth?

Let us also add a tool here that will help you solidify your takeaways for the rest of the book. If you just read through the pages and do not practice, you may remember only about 5 percent of the tips, tools, and insights here. That is a horrible waste of your precious time. If you are not familiar with S.M.A.R.T. goal-setting, let us explore what it is and how it will be useful to you.

(By the way, if you look up S.M.A.R.T. on the Internet, you will find many, many variations. I had to choose one for simplicity here, but find the version that works best for you.)

Here are the basics to start with using one of the many models:

S.M.A.R.T. Goals
S. pecific

M. easurable

A. ctionable

R. elevant

T. ime Bound

Let us use an example involving empathy. Often, people will start to move toward a desired change with self-talk like, "I want to improve empathizing." They think that is a goal. It really is just a nice intention. We call that non-S.M.A.R.T. desire a wish and not a goal. Now let us enhance the probability of your actually succeeding in the direction of empathizing and put S.M.A.R.T. goal setting into play:

Specific: I will find ways to practice empathizing with my friends Peter and Christie.

Measurable: I will look for five instances in each of the next three days to empathize with them.

Actionable: Because I will be seeing Peter and Christie this coming weekend, and because I know what empathy is and have a desire to improve my empathizing, I can indeed take actions to practice.

Relevant: I know that empathizing does bring people together and I want to improve my negotiation relationships, so this is very much relevant to that goal.

Time bound: I will look for these empathizing opportunities this coming weekend starting on Saturday morning, April 6, at 10 a.m. and ending this small pilot test program at 5 p.m. on Monday, April 8.

You can see how clearly this methodology brings more probable success of your goal to improve your empathizing skills.

In all of the chapters following, we strongly recommend that you take the time to anchor your learning with S.M.A.R.T. goal setting. Otherwise, you will retain as little as 5 percent of what you read.

Goals for Success

From the answers you get to the questions above, write S.M.A.R.T. goals that will lead to greater success with mutuality, proactivity, and R.E.S.P.E.C.T.

S.M.A.R.T. Goals for Mutuality, Proactivity, and R.E.S.P.E.C.T. Success

S. pecific

M. easurable

A. ctionable

R. elevant

T. ime Bound

I will _____

2

Reviewing Human Fundamentals

We spend a lot of time on the human factor in this book because it is human beings who are negotiating. And we humans are complex, adding lots of additional ingredients to the negotiating process beyond just the nuts and bolts of bargaining. People negotiate with people. The unique feature of this book is that you come away with many, many more tools on what is called the *soft* side of negotiations, even as we spend lots of time on the hard skills, too. Remember, *soft* definitely does not mean *easy*.

We cover some fundamental aspects of (professional) human beings here and build on some of the topics in later chapters, too. The realms we talk about when viewing complex human beings are the mental, emotional, physical, social, and even spiritual factors. If you have not considered all of these contributions of people in negotiations before, stay tuned and look for the value-add to your knowledge and practice sets.

Mental/emotional: There is a lot of mental activity in the negotiations process. But mental activity does not occur in a vacuum, whether internal to oneself or combined with the mental activity of the other party. Let us take a first high-level look at some internal dynamics at play within people (see Figure 2.1).

Neurons and dendrites: What does this mean? The gray and white matter of our brain is largely made up of neurons. They can

FIGURE 2.1   Internal Dynamics at Play

be viewed for us laypeople as storage units and cells for potential activity. The latest scientific studies say we average 86 billion neurons in the human brain. Lots anyway. Dendrites, described as *neuronal arms*, are strands that connect neurons and allow them to talk with each other.

Thoughts and feelings: The activity we are concerned with here regarding neurons and dendrites is what we call *thoughts* and *feelings*. We view our thoughts as streams of information. We have about 60,000 to 70,000 thoughts a day. The scary part is that most of these thoughts are the same day after day after day. The good news is that neuroscience and psychology are clear that we have a good degree of control on what thoughts we have. The bad news is that changing our thoughts to become more positive and productive takes work. That is just the way it is. But that is the opportunity for all of us who want better lives (and better negotiations).

Our thoughts send a chemical message to the body and we experience these messages as feelings or emotions. For instance, during a negotiation, if you have thoughts of possibility—from a mental perspective—things are going well and the chemical response in our body is one of feeling good. If you are negotiating with someone who is clearly trying to take advantage of you, your thoughts of wariness will produce a different chemical and you will experience different feelings/emotions, perhaps anger or resentment. (We talk in Chapter 3 about how to use this information to your advantage.)

Actions: If your neurons and dendrites are producing positive thoughts and feelings in a negotiation, your actions will tend to be those that continue the positive interactions you are creating. If you have negative thoughts and feelings (like wariness), your actions will reflect that. You will probably start holding back information. If the other party is using negative tactics against you, you may start acting that way, too. Unless you are leading from the higher ground, one negative action leads to another.

Results: Our actions (or inaction) produce our results. In other words, results do not lie. They are what they are. So the results of positive actions produced by positive thoughts and feelings will most likely be outcomes that you say are at least "good enough," or win-win. If your actions are fueled by negativity, the results may perhaps look okay in the short term, but in the long run, when dealing with the same party again, they will probably come back to bite you. People do not forget negative negotiations. Previous negative sessions will be the starting point for future negotiations, which is not a good way to begin.

To be a mutuality-based, long-term win-win negotiator, then, there will certainly be changes to make for better and better results. You are human and no one is perfect. We can all get better (and produce ever better results). The beauty of the fact that results do not lie is that you can evaluate your outcomes anytime you choose. Then you can work your way back up the chart. Did you get results that are not good enough for your goals? What actions (or inaction) did you take to get those results? Then, continuing to move back up through the process, what thoughts

FIGURE 2.2   The New Internal Dynamics at Play

and feelings did you have that guided your actions? And when you decide (to begin at least) to change your thoughts and feelings, your neurons and dendrites begin to rewire (generally figure on 21 to 90 days to begin to change habitual thoughts/feelings). We talk further about evaluation in Chapter 15 as a purposeful way of including this process.

Figure 2.2 shows what the new you will look like.

If you are wise, you will consciously, purposely use this cyclical evaluating change process for life and for your greater good. Your negotiation results will improve, too.

False Self and True Self

Added to the physiological, biological, and chemical factors of being a human involved in negotiations, another highly influential ingredient in all human interactions—professional and personal—is what is called the *mind*. Unless you have had the additional background of counseling, coaching, and so on, offered to you in the writing of this book, it is unlikely that your academic or professional training has acquainted you well enough with the inner landscape we tackle next.

What the mind *is* has many explanations and components. We delve into a side of the mind and a side we loosely call *heart*. There is an aspect of the mind—a very powerful aspect—that has its own agenda and, when active, usually produces negative thoughts, feelings, and actions. So the results are negative, too. This side of us goes by many names, including the *naysayer*, the *complainer*, the *judger*, the *blamer*, and the *saboteur*. Not inspiring labels, are they? Because many specialists call it the *ego*, we use that title to refer to all the names collectively. And together they are called the *false self*. While this aspect of mind is indeed part of us, it is only a small fraction of our total make-up. But the ego/false self can be very powerful. It can take over our thinking, feelings, and actions for a while. And that can be dangerous. In effect, it pretends to be us (falsely) and the results are usually negative.

On the other hand, we call our higher side the *heart* or *true self*. Some of the names that different disciplines call this are: *higher self*, *divine self*, *source*, *Christ consciousness*, *Buddha nature*, *spirit*, *wise self*, *universal self*, and many more. In this tricky human thing about "what we are," these names refer to the essence of our being. Kind of elusive, isn't it. But here is a basic way of understanding the difference between false self and true self: false self helps produce ultimately negative effects, and true self helps produce positive results.

We look more deeply at how to recognize when the false self or true self are running the show in Chapter 3, "Expanding Emotional Intelligence."

Let us get back to the false self. The ego's main purpose is to keep us safe, which sounds good and is a fine thing for our basic survival. The problem is that the ego will do anything it feels it has to in order to keep us safe. And safety for the ego is usually about emotional safety. Think about many if not most negotiations. They can be filled with uncomfortable moments of emotion. So to fulfill its mission of emotional safety, the ego plays what is called the *Right/Wrong Game*, which means I am right and you are wrong—essentially win-lose. It makes sense, then, to see that the ego is the instigator of all conflict. While we more fully cover conflict in Chapter 6, let us see how the ego contributes to malfunctioning instead of healthy disagreement in life and therefore in negotiations.

Let us take a look at one of the sources of conflict—*missing information*. In a negotiation, information used wisely is power. So when information is missing, there is a lack of power. The ego likes power and not a lack of power. If, for instance, it is discovered that there is missing information from the other party, the ego may jump in and react. The reaction may be to "blame" you. Where neutral curiosity from our *true self* would serve a more peaceful and productive negotiation, the blamer now has an egoic mission of making you right and the other party wrong. It has little interest in whether the missing information is intentional or simply human error. It assumes and projects the intention of playing unfairly onto the other party. So conflict ensues.

If noticing these inner dynamics are new to you, no worries. If you recognize how important it is to differentiate the two opposing inner pieces of you, perhaps you will study this further. If you do, your life (and your negotiations) will absolutely change for the better.

Physical: Now that we have covered some mental/emotional aspects to being a human and a negotiator, we spend just a little time on the physical.

You: It is critical that you are in top form when money and reputations are on the line. Because your body (including your brain) is the host from which you engage in negotiations, it makes sense to have that body in the best health. Attending to our physical welfare often takes a backseat in these days of increased professional pressures. But that just makes matters worse. The simple cause and effect are that if you do not eat well, your body cannot perform to its highest potential. If you do not get enough overall rest, and especially before key negotiations, your mind and body will not be fully up to the task. If you do not regularly work your many muscle groups, your negotiating muscles will suffer, too. Inconsequential? The opposite is true. What is in it for you to take better care of yourself? Everything!

Other: You are not in charge of the physical health of the other negotiating party. But it does make sense to add their physical health to your radar list. If you are not in top form and they are, they will have the advantage; be sharper and stronger. If their physical health is compromised, you need to determine how that may compromise the negotiating process. In mutuality-based negotiations, we care about the other person(s) because we know that it takes two to tango. You are a negotiating "partner." Every negative thing that goes on for them may also affect you negatively. So be more aware of their state of health so you can counter any imbalance they may be working from.

Physical environmental factors: Your surroundings impact you mentally, emotionally, and physically. If you have not given this previous thought, now is the time to begin. Everyone has different physical needs, different comfort zones. If you are too warm or cold, how does that affect your or their ability to be at your sharpest? If the chairs are uncomfortable, how does that distraction or fatigue-producer influence activities and outcomes? Do you need more sunlight? Many people suffer from some degree of SAD (Seasonal Affective Disorder) and do not even know it. We have become so used to working in sterile environments that the negative consequences are no longer part of our consciousness. Know yourself well and negotiate the environmental needs in advance for being at your best.

You also need to watch out for people who manipulate the environment. When negotiating in person, where are you conducting the meetings? Site selection is important. Are you on your home turf? On their home grounds? Have you negotiated a neutral place? What will work best for win-win outcomes? Professionals who negotiate frequently and have been trained to be manipulative, win-lose operators may try to set up environmental conditions that have an adverse effect on you. Do not sit on the other side of *their* desk. Do not allow them to sit in a higher seat than you. Do not allow their incoming phone calls to disrupt proceedings (the calls may be preplanned). In general, stay alert for any environmental condition that places more power on either side. Use environment for the greater good.

Social: We cover two major aspects of the social factors in Chapters 3, 4, and 5, but let us just set the stage here. *Social* means degrees of interaction between or among people. Negotiations qualify, so human basics are involved here. What behavioral styles have come together in a negotiation session? How great is the gap between styles? People of different ages will generally approach things differently. Men and women have some trends that set them apart from each other. Cultural differences can have a major role in separating negotiators (never a good thing). Levels of education may be a gap factor. Because these topics are each a special study area, we simply point out here that they exist and suggest that you note what you need to further study for your increased success.

Spiritual: Out in the world, this one has lots of confusion to it. This definition works well for our purposes: "Of, relating to, or affecting the human spirit or soul as opposed to material or physical things." Unlimited volumes of books have been written within all manner of disciplines about the human spirit. Let us agree to use it here as *the energy that fuels people's lives*; therefore, negotiators' lives, too. Have you ever walked into a room and even though you did not witness what went on between two people, you can feel the argument that just occurred? Or someone walks into a room and everyone seems to light up just a little more. You are feeling the energy. Science now knows that the "solid" world we all see with our limited human eye is a kind of illusion—99.9999 percent of everything is energy. A mere 0.0001 percent of the universe is matter or particles (solid).

What matters about this subject is how your energy is in relationship to the other negotiating party's energy. Are you "kindred spirits"? Do you get along so naturally that you are in instant ease when negotiating with this person? Or at the other extreme, do they simply "rub you the wrong way"? People are usually somewhere in between with each other. Again, it is a matter of degree. But this is an important factor—if your emotional intelligence is high, you will be aware of the state of spirit or energy between you from the start. If you are at ease with each other, everything else is likely to unfold more smoothly.

What do you do, though, when you notice that you simply "feel" at odds with the other? If there were no apparent actions that felt wrong, actions that can be corrected, then the first step is acknowledging the unease to yourself. If you are more courageous, you might even name the feeling out loud to the other person. Unspoken elephants in the room can do damage. However, that will be your call. If you notice incompatible energies, rising above that and finding common ground elsewhere within the person or in the physical realm can help. You can actively look for qualities or character traits that are in alignment with your own. Celebrate those. You can simply focus on the goods or services being exchanged, looking for a win-win outcome even if you do not "like" the person's energy (different from personality differences that we cover in Chapter 4). The more you discover about the energetic or spirit force within you, the very essence of who and what you are, the more you can use this awareness when in the energy fields of others.

Centricities

As you are learning, human beings have more complexity than many people acknowledge. Every aspect that shows up in the professional who you negotiate with, that you miss, can cause trouble. The better you get at identifying the many human aspects at play, the more likely you are to proactively use that knowledge to mutual advantage.

Centricity is another core component of being human. What is *centric*? The definition I like best for our purposes here is: "centered upon, focused around." It is a rare human being who focuses more on others than himself (even if subconsciously). Our blueprinting, our neurons and dendrites, our thoughts, feelings, and actions all begin at home within us in human form. We therefore begin centric.

What are people's natural centric defaults? Male and female, age, culture, language, spirituality (religion or otherwise), geography, education, industry, company, and on and on. . . . Every one of these areas can either be a gap-producer or a place of common ground. But you first have to notice your own centricities and then also notice the other's centric defaults.

Let us take company-centric, for example. Look at your own life. You likely go to the same building, the same office every day. You probably take the same modes of transportation and same routes on a regular basis. In working with your teammates, you probably use similar language (buzzwords) and the environment becomes subliminally memorized. That "Is Your World," so to speak. If you are negotiating internally, you will have lots of common ground with your company partners even though there may still be problematic gaps in department, age, gender, skill-set . . . centricities.

When you interact with (negotiate with) professionals outside of your company, your daily routines, your regularly reinforced knowing-base, and so on, conditions are ripe for differences. Differences are the fodder for conflict. To be successful with those outside of your world(s), you need to meet them where *they* are. We call this the *Platinum Rule* when we get to Chapter 4 and negotiating styles. Their own world, their own centricities run their thinking, feelings, and acting systems unless they are more enlightened and emotionally intelligent than most. It is your job to be proactive in taking the lead on this vast subject. You need to observe your own areas of centric. You need to see how yours differs from theirs. You need to encourage greater communication to understand where each of you is coming from to bridge the gap.

Reviewing Human Fundamentals Summary

We are mental, emotional, physical, social, and spiritual beings. All of these factors are in motion when we are negotiating, whether you are aware of that or not. Paying more attention to all five realms will absolutely give you an advantage in leading the way to mutuality-based, win-win negotiations. Paying attention to common ground and gaps in what is centric to yours and the other's lives will also open possibilities for more success.

Questions to Ponder
- What will it be like to see myself as having five contributing realms?
- How will it serve me to pay more attention to my thoughts?
- What do I tend to do when emotions run high?
- What are the outcomes when my thoughts and feelings are negative?
- What results occur when my thoughts and feelings are positive?
- What are my negotiations like when I am feeling physically strong?
- What impact does feeling less than my best have on my negotiations?
- What are my social strengths and weaknesses?
- How can I (over time) turn social weaknesses around?

- What is the fuel within me called *spirit*?
- How do I feel the energy of any and all other persons?
- What can I do for better outcomes when I don't "feel" right with someone?
- What are my most ingrained centricities?
- How might my centricities limit my thinking, feeling, and acting?

Goals for Success

From the answers you get to the questions earlier, write S.M.A.R.T. goals that will lead to greater success with your human fundamentals.

S.M.A.R.T. Goals Regarding Human Fundamentals
S. pecific
M. easurable
A. ctionable
R. elevant
T. ime Bound
I will _____

3

Expanding Emotional Intelligence

You have all heard of IQ (Intelligence Quotient). This is a common and prized way of assessing a human being. Classical assessments are delivered in many school systems, and the corporate world places a high emphasis on intellectual intelligence. There is nothing inherently wrong with that, but it is an incomplete way of viewing a human being, personally or professionally.

In my many humanistic training experiences and with my 25 years in the corporate world, I have come to understand that human beings are much more than just their intellect. So it will be helpful for you to view the people you negotiate with as having five major realms: mental (IQ included), emotional, physical, spiritual, and social. If this takes you aback at first, it is probably only because this is a new way of looking at humans, professional or otherwise. But science, business, and psychology are constantly expanding what they know about people. These years, to be successful we all need to be in constant learning and expansion mode.

If you are like the rest of us, negotiating used to be considered a set of hard skills only. But as we mentioned earlier in this book, "negotiating success" comes from dealing with hard skills that have soft edges. The field of emotional intelligence

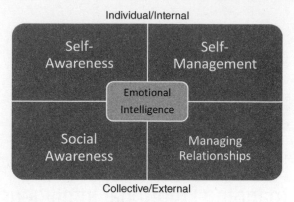

FIGURE 3.1   The Four Basic Areas of EQ

(also known as EQ) will certainly be classified as one of soft skills. The word *soft* does no justice to the difficulty involved in mastering EQ. Be forewarned that increasing your EQ might be the greatest challenge of your life. However, the professional and personal rewards from an expanded emotional intelligence will be well worth all of your efforts. And these efforts will be a lifelong journey.

Let's begin to unpack some of the most vital components of EQ and relate the pieces to the negotiating process. The four basic areas, as seen in Figure 3.1, are self-awareness, self-management, social awareness, and managing relationships.

Each of the four quadrants has its own set of components to work on, and expanding any single area in your own life will bring many rewards. But none of the four quadrants operates in a vacuum; they are all interconnected. The four quadrants can be separated into two connecting halves. The top two— self-awareness and self-management—are all about you the individual. The bottom two halves address you in relationships with other people. Most human beings do not live in isolation, but instead, interact with other people. This is certainly the case in negotiating. Still, it is helpful to address each of the four areas one by one.

Self-Awareness

Let's start with the first quadrant, self-awareness. What is this thing we call *self-awareness*? It sounds so simple. Try this for a moment: Close your eyes and slowly count to five at about one numeral per second. Did you count to five? What part of you noticed that you were counting to five? It was not the counter; that was busy counting. There was another part of you, called by different names, that was aware of your counting. Some call this the *Observer*. Other disciplines call it the *Witness*. Whatever you want to call it, it is a part of the mind that has awareness. It is this aspect of you that is your greatest ally in becoming more self-aware.

Thinking: What can we ask the Observer to observe? Let us start with thoughts. You can call your counting from one to five, *thoughts*. We have said that you have 60,000 to 70,000 a day. Over the course of your life to date, on a day-to-day basis, how many of these thoughts are you actually aware of? For most of us, these thoughts, at 700 to 800 per minute, zip in and out under our awareness radar. In fact, neuroscience says that most of the 60,000 to 70,000 thoughts a day are the same day after day after day. That is pretty scary. And having the same thoughts over and over again is a trap. Traps do not serve the negotiation process, nor do they help us get better as a negotiator.

Here is a phrase you might use: "I have thoughts, but I am not my thoughts." This one can be particularly confusing. School systems, parents, and the business world are deeply entrenched in thinking. Again, thinking is all well and good. But when prized above all other aspects of being a human being, its incompleteness ultimately leads to failure. You are much more than just your thoughts. We come back to the positives and negatives of thinking in the negotiation process after we have explored some of the other aspects of self-awareness.

Feelings: Let us look at "feelings" next—feelings as equated to emotion (we discuss feeling as physical sensation later).

Your emotions can be viewed as messengers. What does that mean? It means that emotions are responses to our thoughts and perceptions. They actually occur immediately in response to a thought; in a nanosecond, really. But if you are like many of us, you are probably not 100 percent in touch with your emotions. From science to psychology the view is that we are *always* in the state of some emotion. The key, then, in the EQ quadrant of self-awareness is to become ever more conscious of your current emotional state. This takes lots of practice, but you will soon see why this will become more and more important to you. Let us take a deeper look into what are considered positive and negative emotions.

The following list contains feelings or emotions that we have when our (negotiation) needs are *not* being met:

Suspicious	Fatigued
Annoyed	Miserable
Angry	Discouraged
Dislike	Uneasy
Confused	Tense
Disconnected	Vulnerable
Embarrassed	Envious

Let's see how a negative emotion might play out in a negotiation. The example we play with for emotions in negotiations is "discouraged." Imagine that you have been in a negotiation for a while and you have an increasing sense of dissatisfaction with how your negotiating partner is behaving. Your every intention has been to create a mutuality-based, win-win relationship. But the other party has clearly demonstrated that they want to get more from you than they are willing to give in reciprocal concessions. Your attempts to encourage a more even exchange have failed. If you tune in to your emotional state about this unequal dynamic, you might notice the feeling of "discouragement."

Because it is true that we are always in a state of emotion, you can probably look around your life and remember times when you or someone else was clearly feeling something but did not use that information to improve things. Lots of people get discouraged in negotiations. If they are not using their EQ, the emotion (in this case, discouragement) will be a negative feeling that guides negative thoughts and negative actions that produce negative results. But there is a higher EQ way of handling things.

Let's say that you are actually aware of the feeling of discouragement. Discouragement is a clear messenger reinforcing that mutuality-based negotiation is not taking place in the way that feels good to you. As soon as you notice this more clearly, you can stop the negotiation. (Later on in this book you will learn to use the Discovery Phase to set up agreements at the start of the negotiation, which allows you to stop for this very kind of intervention.) You can take a break for yourself to list the factors that contribute to your discouragement. Or, if your relationship with the other negotiating party is solid enough, you can explore your negative feelings directly with them. Either path you choose, you are paying attention to the emotion of discouragement. Not overriding or bypassing that feeling gives you more opportunity to change the course of the process for more positive outcomes. How does this example make sense to you?

We used discouragement as a single example of what often shows up in negotiations. But each of the negative feelings listed earlier are messengers or warning signs that tell you that things are not going the way you would like. The corrective process regarding any and all of them is to notice the feeling, pause and explore what the emotion is telling you, and see what you, can do to eliminate whatever has been causing that emotion.

Let us turn our attention to what are considered positive feelings, positive emotions. The following are feelings or emotions that we have when our (negotiating) needs *are* being met:

Warm	Inspired
Engaged	Pleased
Optimistic	Thrilled
Confident	Peaceful
Excited	Refreshed
Grateful	

Like the negative emotions we discussed, positive emotions are also messengers. When these are present within you, they are indicators that the negotiation process is unfolding in ways that are satisfying to you. Unlike the negative emotions in which we suggest pausing the negotiation to turn the negativity around, feeling a positive emotion is not a lengthy interruption. When you feel positivity, you may choose to reinforce the good feeling by telling your negotiations partners what they are doing to contribute. (When you get to negotiation styles later in the book, you will begin to learn how to give any feedback—negative or positive—situationally based on style.)

We can use the same basic phrasing mentioned earlier regarding thoughts and say, "I have feelings, but I am not my feelings." Objectively, this is easy to say and basically true. But can you recall a time when an emotion has been so strong for you, so overwhelming that it really takes over your life for that bit of time when it is active. A colleague of mine relates about a time when she became so angry at her mother that the two almost came to blows. She says that she can't even remember what they argued about. But the emotion was so strong as to be unforgettable. When it comes to negotiating, strong negative emotions can certainly destroy the current negotiation and potentially the relationship for future negotiations with the same party.

To deepen your understanding of this, let's take a look at the physiological forces involved in severe emotions, particularly anger. It is simply true that most of us have times when we are with people—in this case, negotiators—with whom we do not see eye-to-eye. It is always a matter of degree, but it is helpful to understand within the subject of negotiating how to anticipate and work through the instances when negative, destructive emotions run high. A major physical player within us is the amygdala.

The amygdala is actually two almond-shaped portions of the middle brain. Although it has numerous functions too biologically complex to spend time with here, it is also called *the seat of emotion*. You have probably heard of the term *fight or flight*. This comes from the amygdala being an ancient aspect of human beings. A high benefit of its function is to help us get through times of danger. In the early days of humankind, that danger might have been a saber-toothed tiger. These days, as sometimes in negotiations, the danger is more often emotional. Unfortunately, the amygdala does not know the difference. The easiest way to understand what happens in what is called an *amygdala hijack* is that the brain/mind receives signals that a threat is at hand. (In the case of negotiations the threat could be a particularly stubborn, obnoxious, loud-spoken bully of a negotiator.)

Think back to the saber-toothed tiger, and imagine the cavemen and women who might have been standing around the fire when they realized the presence of this formidable and ravenous beast. Now imagine that Og looked up and said, "My, my, look at the size of that fella. He must have a record-length tail. And aren't those the biggest canines you've ever seen." Well, by that time, Og had become the tiger's dinner. What saved the Ogs of the world more times than not was the amygdala's ability to suspend our normal filtering conscious thinking and put ourselves into survival mode. In Og's case, the fight-or-flight mechanism would likely have resulted in either his raising the spear to confront the tiger or running like heck to the greater safety of the cave.

What the amygdala does to accomplish the cessation of circumspective thought is to shoot the chemical cortisol into our filtering center of consciousness, our frontal lobe. This is like having the dentist use lidocaine anesthetic to numb your gum and tooth. Our thinking is numbed. Again, obviously not a good state of mind ever, but particularly not when negotiating. One easy way to remember this process is to remember, "When emotions are high, intelligence is low." Although you are reminded of the amygdala hijack factor in Chapter 6, "Dissolving Conflict," let's take a couple more moments on how to catch the hijack early or reduce its impact if it becomes full blown.

If you're in a negotiation and a relationship in communication starts to heat up, it is ideal to be aware of the rising emotions sooner rather than later. The less cortisol that goes into the frontal lobe, the more intelligent you will be in finding ways to dissolve the conflict early. The chemical component of an amygdala hijack has physiological truths. The more cortisol that is pumped out, the longer it takes to come back to a peaceful, centered state of mind. And if you do not clear enough of the chemical cortisol out of your brain before continuing the negotiation, it does not take much to retrigger the hijack. What do you do about this? Three possible solutions (using all three is best) are, first, to take a break as soon as you feel yourself getting triggered (or notice the other party getting triggered). The length of the break that you negotiate depends on how high the emotions have run (how much cortisol is in your brain or the other party's brain). The second intervention is to drink lots of noncaffeinated fluids, effectively flushing the cortisol out of your system. The third activity that you can use is to move your body rapidly enough that your heart beats faster and again hastens the process of flushing. Depending on where you are, heartbeat-raising activities could be taking a brisk walk, going to a private space and doing any kind of callisthenic, from jumping jacks to deep-knee bends. So ideally, you would take a break, drink lots of fluids, and find a way to exercise for a few minutes before reentering an important negotiation.

Body sensations: Another key area of self-awareness is noticing your body sensations. You might be asking yourself "What the heck do body sensations have to do with negotiating my product or service?" There is a phrase that might help you: "The body never lies." When we are tuning into ourselves, being in self-awareness, it is helpful to view the body as another messenger of what is going on within us. Our thoughts are contained within the body part we call the *brain*. Our feelings are actually a chemical experience within our bodies that we call *emotions*. But these two sources also result in body sensations. For instance, where do you feel anger? Where in your body do you feel fear? Some of you will have an immediate, clear answer. But like many of us, you may not have been taught to recognize your body sensations as indicators of what is going on outside you and within you.

Here is an example of how tuning in to your body sensations can be your ally. Let us say that you are more and more practiced at listening to what your body tells you as you go into your next important negotiation. Imagine you have put an offer on the table and the response is what we would call a *manipulative tactic* (much more to come about tactics later in the book). Although you may be hearing the words of the tactic (and the tactic is always meant to put you in a weakened position), if you were listening to your body's response to being put into a weakened position, you might get clear more quickly that you are being put at a disadvantage and find ways to confront and eliminate that tactic. How might your body be giving you the signals? What might you be feeling for? You might relate a tactic to an attack. You might feel your jaw tense when attacked. You might experience an increased heart rate. Perhaps you feel a discomfort in your solar plexus. Whatever goes on in your body, you will eventually have a practice of using that information to your advantage. So body sensations can indeed become a stronger, more powerful ally in the negotiations of life.

Here is an example from of a body sensation that became apparent in one of my negotiations. I was a nursing home administrator; the vice president of the hospital group I worked for and I were one negotiating team. We were working on creating a contract with the union. During the negotiation process that lasted many months, the two of us would show up for the Tuesday night sessions to find four to seven negotiating members on the union's side—clearly a power tactic. But I was young and inexperienced at lengthy, formal negotiations. I felt overwhelmed in each and every session. Looking back, I did not realize at the time how my body was clearly telling me of my perceived disadvantage. I can remember having a constant gnawing sensation in my gut. If I had tuned in to the bodily discomfort, I would have read the inequity more clearly. If I had observed my thoughts ("this is so uneven"), felt my emotions (overwhelm and fear), and clearly felt my gut's response to that, it might have been clear that a new strategy was needed. But I did not. I allowed those unfavorable dynamics to continue for the entire length of the complex negotiation. The resulting contract was not favorable. What would you have done differently if you had been more self-aware of these thoughts, feelings, and body sensations? What steps might you have taken early on from that information?

Self-awareness includes these three big areas of thoughts, feelings, and body sensations. But there are additional areas for you to pay attention to: your judgments, beliefs, intuitions, and impulses. The more you use your "Observer Self" to notice all of your inner facets, the more you can use the information to either continue what you are doing or adjust your actions depending on the results you are getting. I hold that you can never get too masterful at being self-aware.

Self-Management

Self-awareness is the starting point for any change you want to make within yourself. If you are not aware, you are blind. But as you get ever more self-aware (I recommend for life), what do you do with all that information? Have you ever been around some-body who clearly was not managing themselves very well? Per-haps you were in a meeting when colleagues were constantly going on tangents that did not pertain to the topic at hand. Their lack of self-management took the meeting further and further away from the agreed-on agenda. Or maybe you have a family member who seems to say everything he or she is thinking. He or she could go on and on without anyone even being in the room. Or you might have noticed that when people consume too much alcohol or other substances, their self-management filter is compromised.

And what about yourself? Take a moment to recall some things you have done or said that, if you could, you would take back. There were consequences for that lack of self-management.

Let's look at the other side of self-management: successes you achieved when indeed you were able to notice your thoughts, feelings, and body sensations, and you used that information to act more wisely.

The Buddhists call this "Right Thoughts, Right Feelings and Right Actions." An example of lack of self-management comes from my very strict Catholic school days. Many of the nuns I encountered clearly had a lack of control—self-management, if you will. The amount of mental, emotional, physical abuse heaped on myself and the students around me was huge. Yelling and slapping were commonplace. It also seemed automatic or mind-less. I imagine that if these nuns had been taught self-awareness and if they exercised that learning, our school environment would have been much more positive. The nuns, using greater self-awareness, could have explored their own thoughts, feelings, and body sensations to see what the cause was for all of the damaging actions they took. They would have undoubtedly discovered more components in their own lives that were equally negative to the actions they were taking out on us. Their greater self-management would have made a positive difference to me and untold numbers of others. What are examples from your life, where people's lack of self-management caused harm of one sort or another?

How does greater self-management come into play in negotiations? Bring your thoughts and attention to a negotiation or two from your own past. What did the other party do or say that you suspect was a bit rash? These words or actions were not in keeping with an agreed-on intention of mutuality. You suspect, in their heart of hearts, if they could choose again, they would do something different. And what about you? What have you said or done that if you could only take it back, you know the outcomes would be different.

We come back to the EQ interrelationship between self-awareness and self-management. Remember that your thoughts are zipping along at 800 words per minute and that your emotions are always simultaneously present. When your self-aware Observer is on duty, you have choice point after choice point regarding what you will do with the information. Though clock-time says these choice points pass in a moment, the more you practice tuning in, the quicker you get at selecting more favorable actions. Self-management, then, is a matter of conscious choice about what to say or not say or what to do or not do. The results will correspond accordingly.

Social Awareness

Together we have explored the top two quadrants of emotional intelligence, self-awareness, and self-management. These are both about the internal you. But as we know, most of us do not live in isolation; we live, work, and negotiate with people. We have an impact on them and they have an impact on us. There are 7 billion humans on this planet, each with a unique blend of emotional intelligence, you included. When you negotiate with others, you encounter their distinct sets of self-awareness, self-management, social awareness, and ability (or inability) to manage relationships. While you can encourage others to become more emotionally intelligent, your own EQ is always an opportunity to improve.

So why improve your social awareness for negotiations? In fact, what is social awareness? Being more socially aware has you tuning in to the clues that people around you are showing. These major indicators of what is going on inside them are often called *verbal* or *nonverbal*. Both are important. Verbal clues are the words you are hearing. Nonverbal clues include facial expressions, body posture, hand signals, and tone of voice. These indicators are present in all people and will certainly be there to notice in your negotiation partners.

How can you begin to put social awareness to better use? I said earlier that what you practice anywhere, you can practice everywhere. And the more you practice anything (and practice it well), the better you get at using your growing expertise when you want to—in this case, in negotiations.

If you wait until you are in a formal negotiation to practice, it is unlikely you will be very good when you need to be. Where else in your life can help you become better at social awareness? Take any relatively close relationship you have. Let us take your boss, for example. Like every other human, he or she is giving out clues all the time. Bosses usually have quite a bit of "Doer" behavior in them (you will learn more about doers later in this book, along with negotiating styles). Behavior can be observed. So a major ingredient in social awareness, the clues that people give off, are observable. If you walked into your boss's work space with your social awareness radar at a heightened level, you would take in the look on his or her face, the tone of voice, and body language. Is your boss's face more open or more closed? More stern or more pleasant? Some people (in this case, your boss) have what we call a *monoface* or *poker face*. Expressionless and very hard to read what is going on for them. We do our best to read facial expressions as an indicator of mood or state of being.

What might you see in your boss's body language? Is he sitting upright and rather stiff? Are his hands flat on his desk and not expressive? Or perhaps he is leaning back in his chair and looking quite comfortable. His hands and arms might be gesturing in friendly fashion. And what of his tone of voice? Are the words carried with flat sharpness? Or is there a warmer undertone to his delivery? All of these are clues for your social awareness to consider. Do you understand that with reading the multiple signals coming from others, you can make better choices as to how you respond?

The same ability to read clues is an essential ingredient in being a successful negotiator. What is going on for the other party? Are they in more positive or negative flow? Do you find them encouraging mutuality, resisting, or somewhere in between? For instance, if your social awareness reads that the other party is in any way troubled, it gives you an opportunity to explore the underlying forces. If you just soldiered on, despite the signals, it is possible you are sabotaging the results.

Example: The Wince

There is a tactic known as the *wince*. The wince is exactly what it sounds like. The person you are negotiating with purposefully uses a recoiling head motion to give you the impression of negative surprise. You have put an offer on the table and he is giving you a physical clue to say that it is not acceptable. As you learn in the chapter on tactics, this may be genuine surprise or an attempt to get you to knee-jerk react in offering another concession. Either way, the wince relies on your social awareness for its effectiveness.

Another area to heighten in your social awareness when negotiating is to listen to changes in tone of voice. Awareness of tone is important in face-to-face negotiating and is even more critical when negotiating by phone. (*Caution*—visual and vocal clues for greater social awareness are absent when negotiating by email.) Lack of visual and vocal clues is why we absolutely recommend negotiating in person if possible, and by phone as a second choice. Attempting to use social awareness when reading email fails because it depends on the receiver to guess at the meaning behind the words, which is clearer when taking in visual and vocal components.

As you'll soon learn, you are able to use tone of voice as a part of assessing someone's behavior quadrant. Some negotiators use a hard voice and hard face in a very strong negotiating style. More mutuality-based negotiators will typically have more inflection carried by warmer tones. While the hard nuts and bolts of negotiating will be the same no matter the personal style, the use of social awareness gives you the information needed to help you understand how to better relate to the other party.

If you happen to be involved in team negotiations, social awareness takes on a more complex nature. You will now need to expand your radar to take in all of the varying personal behaviors and negotiating styles. If you pay strong attention to the clues given off by the members of the other negotiating team, you will better understand when they are in harmony or not. These clues will help you decide where to probe to clarify the other team's collective challenges and opportunities. Good relationships reduce conflict and improve results.

The same social awareness is critical to use if *you* are part of a negotiating team. Even if you have done proper and complete team preparation, and everyone seems to know their roles and defined areas of contribution, people will still be people. For instance, one of your team member's self-management is not strongly developed. He or she may interject something at an inappropriate time. If you have preagreed with your team members on a way to handle what could look like a disjointed team, your social awareness to recognize straying from alignment will become useful.

You can now see how social awareness is a logical next step in the process of expanding your emotional intelligence. Self-awareness is the job of each human being, each professional in the negotiating process. Although self-awareness is something strictly hidden within you and every other negotiating partner you will ever have, self-management, or the lack thereof, becomes more evident to you and those around you when social awareness is used to detect managed or unmanaged behavior. All three emotional intelligence quadrants covered so far do work together. But they are incomplete without the fourth and last quadrant, "Managing Relationships."

Managing Relationships

In the ordinary life of ordinary people, relationships between and among others is fairly haphazard. Relationship-building and the essential use of emotional intelligence is unfortunately not commonly known yet. But it is a growing field. You are now well on your way to becoming more of a leader and conscious determiner of the kind of relationships you build.

In win-lose negotiating, there is much less or no need to pay attention to building a positive relationship. Win-lose negotiating is transactional; only this single negotiation counts. But more often than not there are potential future negotiations at stake with any negotiating partner. You play win-lose negotiating at your own peril. The old expression "cutting off your nose to spite your face" is what you are doing.

So let's assume that you are a more enlightened negotiator, always striving for win-win outcomes. To achieve mutually positive results, you need to be strong in managing relationships. The clues you have gained about yourself through self-awareness, and the results you have achieved through self-management both contribute positively to managing relationships. And the process of managing relationships will be a constant component from the very beginning to the very end of all bargaining sessions. Relating never stops. It either goes well, not well, or somewhere in between. Can you see how important this is?

For example, let's say you are negotiating a car at a dealership. You have done solid preparation before coming on to the lot. A salesperson (happens to be a man) approaches you and your awareness is heightened. From the very first moment of seeing and hearing this sales pro, you are actively taking in his clues. You are also self-assessing how your own thoughts, feelings, and body sensations are responding to the salesman's presence.

Your first inclination is to label this dealership rep as *sleazy*. You have the stereotypical used car salesman in front of you. What are the clues you have observed in making this initial assessment? Because you used the visual clues of social awareness, you noticed his face change from neutral to a big old grin as he approached you. When you were still 10 feet away from each other, his arm was out with a hand extended for a hearty handshake. His tone of voice was a few decibels louder than that of normal conversation. He simply glowed with friendliness. Given that this is the first time you have met this gentleman, you really do not know his true nature. But what you have guessed about him so far is worth exploring. There are hugely friendly and genuine salespeople. They can be highly trustworthy. But you also know that you need to be wary with some people. Your emotional intelligence will help you determine how to proceed from here.

Expanding Emotional Intelligence Summary

Emotional intelligence is a set of awareness and skills that allow you to live, work, and negotiate with greater success and satisfaction. The four major components of EQ are self-awareness, self-management, social awareness, and managing relationships. Each of these four areas has its own set of stand-alone skills and character traits to make them individually effective. But it is when you use all four areas in integrated fashion that you produce the complete product.

Case Study

Throughout the rest of this book, we use this case study to build on and integrate the unfolding topics.

The basic scenario is this. The timing is right to buy a side-by-side duplex as a rental property. You are actively searching. You will live in one side and use the income from the other apartment to help pay for the mortgage.

How will self-awareness, self-management, social awareness, and managing relationships come into play during this investigation and eventual negotiation?

Self-awareness: It will serve you well to notice what you are thinking, how you are feeling, and what your body sensations are telling you as you navigate the process. These are all messengers to listen to closely. If you have made a list of all your must-haves, ideals, preferences, and do-not-wants, your mind, body, and spirit will all be tuned for success. Noticing when you are thinking negative thoughts, experiencing negative emotions, and feeling negative body sensations will all tell you when you are on track for success and fulfillment and when something is off.

Self-management: Buying a rental property (like all purchases) has an emotional component. Master sellers/negotiators know this and will play on your emotions. For instance, if the seller uses the principle of influence called *scarcity*, you may feel a panic if you think someone else will buy the property before you. That panic may have you impulsively going past your bottom line (Chapter 9). This is where self-management comes in. You *can* hold back on impulsive actions.

Social awareness: Actively taking in the clues given by the seller/negotiator will continuously inform you on what you need to do in response or what to be proactive about with them to influence positive outcomes.

Managing relationships: You are in a dance with the rental property seller. It is part of your negotiating job to reduce friction and increase positivity for the seller to deal with you more openly and honestly.

Questions to Ponder

- What is your general current state of emotional intelligence?
- In what ways can you improve your self-awareness?
- What do you need to self-manage for better results?
- In what areas can you improve your social awareness?
- What personal and professional relationships do you currently have that would benefit from better relationship management?

Goals for Success

From the answers you get to the questions above, write S.M.A.R.T. goals that will lead to greater emotional intelligence success.

S.M.A.R.T. Goals for EQ Success
S. pecific
M. easurable
A. ctionable
R. elevant
T. ime Bound
I will _____

4

Working with Negotiating Styles

We just spent significant time exploring emotional intelligence. We know that negotiators often focus almost exclusively on the process, company pressures, and tangibles being traded. What is often forgotten is that negotiations always unfold between and among people. If you are aiming for mutual success, it is critical to understand that you will frequently negotiate/trade with people who act in ways that are different from your own. Studying behavior styles, here showing up as negotiating styles, will definitely further your ability to be a more well-rounded and effective negotiator.

From the time of the Greek physician Hippocrates, 2,500 years ago, until today, it has been helpful to organize and simplify the approach to understanding human behavior. Hippocrates understood that even though everyone is unique in his or her entirety, people have commonalities that link them. He realized that for him to better serve his patients, knowing their preferences might help him to relate to each for greater healing. So he created the first four-quadrant behavior style mode that we know of. And we get to that soon. But let's begin the exploration of why we are on this subject of behavior styles and why these models work.

As I travel globally, I have asked thousands of program participants if they know the Golden Rule. Many will raise their hands and the usual definition they give is: "Do unto others as you would have them do unto you." In more modern language, "Treat others like you would like to be treated." With that mutual understanding, I then ask something like this: "If you went into work every day reminding yourself of the Golden Rule, to treat other people like you want to be treated, do you think that would help your relationships?" With just a little consideration, 98 percent of hands go up. I pause and then tell them how sorry I am that this is how they go about things. Confusion shows in many faces (yes, I set them up).

I then ask them if they know the Platinum Rule. Rarely do I get a yes. The Platinum Rule says to "treat others like *they* want to be treated." The truth is that "they" are most likely not that very much like you. People have different neuron/dendrite wiring and firing, different personalities, different experiences, different ways of processing information, and on and on. If you "assume" that your way of looking at life and doing things is how they do, too, you will be off the mark more often than you are correct.

So we say that you have to "meet them where *they* are" (not where *you* are); apply the Platinum Rule. Think of it this way—if you want people to treat you like you want to be treated, they will need to step away from their own preferences (Golden Rule) and practice the Platinum Rule. Make sense?

What behavior style models or personality indicators can you use? The well-known Myers Briggs indicator (Isabel Briggs Myers and Katherine Cook Briggs) is a brilliant tool for reading human beings. For most people, though, the 16 main factor areas are a bit too complex for casual employment. A four-quadrant model of behavior styles is easier to grasp and useful to learn and employ for negotiations (and for all personal and professional interactions).

But I must caution you that looking at people (negotiators) through the lens of any four-quadrant behavior styles model is simply another useful set of skills for your tool kit. As you have already seen through your own experiences and the preceding chapters, we humans are truly complex creatures. We have neurological programming. We have mental, emotional, physical, social, and spiritual wiring. There are stored beliefs and assumptions at play. Still, using what you can learn by observing people's behavior will give you many clues as to how to negotiate with them more effectively. In this book, we equate "behavior style" with "negotiating style."

There are many four-quadrant models that you can find on the web. Taking full assessments will get you more deeply versed in your own behavior and further you on the road to behavior observation mastery. But what you can learn here will be helpful in getting your feet wet on this critical subject. I personally have taught six different four-quadrant models. The terminology each uses varies but at the heart of them all are the same fundamental ingredients. For ease of remembering, we use the model that labels the four quadrants as Doer, Thinker, Talker, and Guardian. These words capture a general association with each as Doers "do," Thinkers "think," Talkers "talk," and Guardians "guard."

Figure 4.1 shows what the four quadrants look like.

We go into some detail about each quadrant, but let us take a more general approach to begin this new and big topic. First, what do we mean by "behavior"? Behavior is anything that human beings say or do. Behavior is observable. We can see and or hear

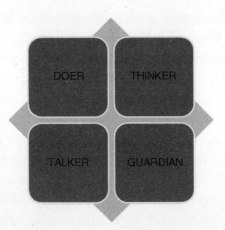

FIGURE 4.1 The Four Behavior Quadrants

what a person is doing. This does *not* tell you why a person is doing what they are doing. We cannot tell their intent from their actions (remember "assuming"?). We do not know what they are thinking, just like no one else can hear the thoughts inside your head. We do not "know" what they feel even as we take in their clues. Still, reading visual, vocal, and verbal clues is a big help (and we address those in Chapter 7). And getting curious and asking powerful questions also helps tremendously in understanding what is going on for the other person (negotiation partner).

Each quadrant's name, then, is a big picture *labeling* of a subset group of specific behaviors—a collective body. It is a rare human who will have all of the behaviors listed within a single quadrant. In fact, the greatest majority of humans have behaviors that are listed in each and every one of the quadrants. We are a blend. Still, many people have what we call a dominant or primary behavior style. That just means that if they were to check off the various specific behaviors listed below, they will likely have a majority of the behaviors checked in a quadrant. They may even have all of them checked but still have a few behaviors checked in other quadrants as well. So calling someone a *Doer* might get you into the trouble of assuming as you clump all Doer behavior into that one person instead of looking to see what other behaviors he or she exhibits.

Staying at the overview level of these behaviors, let's look at some additional useful tendencies. Although each of the four categories has unique behaviors within, there are some general common relationships worth noting. Quadrants that are side by side with each other, neighbors, share some similar attributes. Looking at the model above and going round it clockwise, you can see that Doer and Thinker are neighbors, Thinker and Guardian are neighbors, Guardian and Talker are neighbors, and Talker and Doer are neighbors. They have some common ground between them that can be helpful in building relationships with people who have enough strong behaviors to place them in one of the other boxes.

The real problems come when people are primarily in opposite quadrants: Doer–Guardian and Thinker–Talker. These people simply have less in common with their "opposite." And every distancing aspect between human beings in general and certainly in negotiations is a set-up for disagreement and failure.

Let's come back to common ground and start with Doer–Thinker. (Take all of this with a grain of salt as every human being is different in myriad ways.) Now that you know not to label people as being a Doer, Thinker, Talker, or Guardian, because they are much more than just that, for the sake of ease and fewer words, I am actually going to do just that. But when I say someone is a Doer, it is a conscious shortcut to saying that Doer (in this case) is his or her dominant behavior style.

So commonality . . . Doers and Thinkers "tend to be" *task-oriented*. They like to get right down to business. They do not see the point of social niceties. So they get along that way. These two also tend to be *less expressive* and *less emotional*. You can listen to their voice and notice a lack of pitch/modulation/up-and-down. They tend to be more *monotone* (another clue as to which quadrant you assess them to be in). They also tend toward *monoface*—they use fewer facial expressions. So you cannot read them as clearly as people who show their thoughts and emotions through looks on their face (a disadvantage when negotiating in person and certainly by phone or email).

Next neighbors . . . Thinkers and Guardians are neighbors. The first commonality is that they are both more *highly structured* than high Doers and high Talkers. They think more linearly and are very practical. They also share a need for more *detail* to understand things. These two tend to *ask more questions* as more information helps them fill in the understanding gaps. They are more "we-centric" than their "I-centric" opposites, the Doers and Talkers. Last, both are more *behind the scenes and easygoing* compared to the stronger personalities, the Doers and Talkers. These are clues to understanding the kind of person you are dealing with.

Next neighbors . . . Guardians and Talkers have some special things in common. Both are more *people*-oriented or relationship-based. They want to connect with you the human being before getting down to business. This is opposite of Doers and Thinkers and presents a gap between the two neighbor groups. Talkers and Guardians are more *expressive* (Talkers much more so, Guardians more quietly). In negotiations, this is helpful as you can take in vocal tones and facial expressions more easily to read what is going on inside these folks.

And the last neighbors are Talkers and Doers. They have a few helpful-to-know traits in common. They are both characterized by *strong personas*. You know they are there. They tend to be *faster*. The clues you can observe are that they talk, move, and make decisions faster. They *tell* more than they ask. They are more *I*-centered rather than we-oriented. You can hear this in their sentences: "I want . . . ," I need . . . , " I think . . . ," I feel. . . . " They are also the *poorest listeners*. This makes sense as they are I-centered tellers. Last, they want the *big picture* and *fewer details*.

This is important enough that we take a moment to summarize:

Doers–Thinkers—Task, Less Expressive, Monotone and Face.
Their opposites: Talkers–Guardians—People-Oriented, More Expressive.
Thinkers–Guardians—Easygoing,   Detailed,   "We,"   Ask Questions.
Their opposites: Talkers–Doers—Dominant-Strong Personas, High Level Summary, "I," Tell.

You can see that trying to proceed in negotiations (or in any relationship) as if everyone is the same (or the same as you— Golden Rule) simply will not work for many, many others. You need to bridge the gaps and work with people as they want to be worked with (negotiated with). Relationships are at the heart of every negotiation between and among people. Forget this key factor and your negotiations will be filled with impatience, misunderstanding, conflict. . . .

What to do? Studying the following details about each behavior style will help. Finding online assessments (like the DiSC products) will bring you even more deeply into the practical knowledge of four-quadrant models. And then actively using that information in real life with real people, all the time, will help you assess other negotiators' behavior styles more efficiently and effectively. All this takes time and commitment. But your reputation and profession are at stake in all the negotiations left to come in your future work (and personal) life.

The last major thought before we get you started on studying the specific quadrant sample behaviors is this: To understand what you have in common with your fellow negotiators (from a behavior style point of view) and where the gaps are (producing conflict), you need to know where *you* lie in the model. I highly recommend that you use the information below as a mini-assessment. As you go through each of the four types, put a check mark next to any behavior that fits your concept of yourself (strongly apparent). Then check in with these selections to see if others who know you would agree that these reflect your behavior patterns, too. Whichever box you have the most check marks in, even by one, is considered your dominant or primary behavior. If you have a tie, that is fine. In fact, it shows more probability of your ability to relate to people in those two (or more) quadrants. We build on your answers later in Chapter 7 when we explore specifically how knowing yours and your negotiating partner's behavior styles will color how you tailor your conveying of information to them; your negotiation presentation.

Now let us run through some basic behavioral traits within each quadrant and learn what you need to do when you are with varied negotiators (or your neighbors). Remember, people usually have behaviors in all boxes but may have a dominant or primary box where more of these behaviors are seen and heard. It is a grand mix and matter of degree.

Doer—Task-Oriented

Wants immediate results: These negotiators are fast-paced in many regards. They are impatient with a slow process and therefore may get impatient with you. To meet them where they are, you will need to pick up your own pace. But you will also need to slow them down at times. To do that, they will need to know that there is something in it for them to do so (W.I.I.F.M.).

Makes quick decisions: Again, speed and the accompanying impatience rules. Expect a quick decision to come from them even when you think there is more to discuss. What is in it for them to prolong their decision making—that is your job to uncover.

Takes authority: Remember, Doers and Talkers are strong personalities; some call this dominant. They are very comfortable taking control. The problem with that is that they do not necessarily ask permission for that. You need to establish your own authority and step up your strength in all areas. If they perceive you as weaker than they are, they may very well go for your juggler. Not pretty!

Controlling: They will use lots of "I" statements. They are used to having their way as they steamroll over people throughout their lives. When negotiating, they operate from "What's mine is mine and what's yours is negotiable."

Aggressive: They are not into niceties. Remember, they are task-oriented. People do not count as much as facts and mission do. "Aggressive" is subjective based on how you operate. If you are easygoing, Doers will feel very aggressive. If you are a fellow Doer, it will just feel like business as usual with them.

Wants bottom line: They do not like details. You need it get to the point and quickly with them. Look for signs of impatience or boredom. You are probably providing too much information (even if that makes sense to you).

Poor listener: Again, they are fast and impatient to move along. They are mentally three steps ahead of whatever aspect you are negotiating. With all that mental activity, they will only be tuning in to you with half an ear. Make sure they have heard key points before moving on. Don't "assume" they got it.

Wants big picture: When they feel they have enough information, the big picture, to make a decision and move on, they are done with you. Get good at giving a clear summary. Then, ask what details need to be filled in. If they define what area they need the details in, they are more apt to pay attention (listen) because *they* have expressed interest. If not, they move on with you or without you. This may not make sense to you but it does to them.

Doer Expectations of You—When You Negotiate with Them, Be Prepared

- To be businesslike and to the point.
- To provide support for their ideas, objectives, and conclusions.
- To communicate with competence and efficiency.

Doer—Sample Roles: As You Start to Put Together the Pieces Defining a Doer, You Will Recognize That the Behavior Traits Associated with Them Fit What Is Needed in These Sample Roles

- CEO
- President/Vice President
- Senior Manager
- Middle Manager
- Administrator
- Director
- Team Leader

Negotiating efficacy: Negotiators who are strongly in the Doer quadrant only win 8 percent of mutuality-based negotiations. If you look at the behavior traits above, you can see that they most often will approach bargaining in a win-lose fashion. Remember, they think and operate from, "What's mine is mine and what's yours is negotiable."

These will probably be the most challenging people to lead to mutually beneficial outcomes. You will have to play at your strongest game to succeed. Still, if a negotiator has intelligence and at least a little willingness to change, you may inspire them to recognize the over-time value of win-win negotiations.

Summary

These people are more likely to be fast, task-oriented, tellers, I-centered, and poor listeners.

To be successful with Doers, you should:

- Be punctual.
- Be well prepared.
- Get to the point quickly.
- Reduce or eliminate socialization.
- Keep emotions at bay.
- Give them (beneficial to you) options for deciding.
- Act as quickly as possible.
- Be clear that they heard what you meant.

Thinker—Task-Oriented

Concentrates on detail: The more information, the more detail the better. They make sense of everything through facts, background, reasons and more.

Thinks analytically: They have very strong left brain capabilities. They take everything apart, looking from as many sides as they can. They compare and contrast information.

Checks accuracy: These are people who want you to prove it to them. They dot "i's" and cross "t's." They are the human perfectionists. They want to get things "right" to the nth degree.

Works systematically: They think and act linearly. For things to make sense, they are laid out in a logical, orderly fashion. One step leads to another to another.

Creates diplomacy: They are "we" people. They do not like conflict. They are very even-keeled and work best in calm situations.

Adheres to standards: In their world, standards or rules make sense. They believe that if one follows the standards, things are more likely to turn out correctly.

Needs more time: Because they ask more questions to get more information so that they have more facts to consider, it makes sense that they need more time to accomplish all of that.

Thinker Expectations of You
- That you will be specific and thorough.
- That you are an expert in the field.
- That your communication and personal work is thorough, precise, and based on accurate facts.

Thinker—Sample Roles
- Accounting
- IT
- Engineering
- Research
- Attorney
- Analyst

Summary

Thinker negotiators win approximately 64 percent of mutuality-based negotiations. They have by far the best records. They tend to be task-oriented, act more slowly, be more easygoing, less emotionally expressive, ask more questions, live "we"-centered and be somewhat better listeners.

Thinker negotiators achieve mutuality-based results because they are extremely thorough, we-based, think long term, are more harmonious, and like to play fair. Playing fair can be a downside in that they "assume" that the other party will also play fair and not everybody does. They tend to be more quickly disclosing giving concessions away without getting concessions in return.

To negotiate successfully with Thinkers, you should:

- Be fully prepared.
- Present facts.
- Deliver lots of detail.
- Organize linearly.
- Be nonconfrontational.
- Invite their left brain creativity.
- Give them time to process.
- Push gently to avoid their analysis paralysis.

Talker—People-Oriented

Socializes conversationally: These are gregarious people. They like to connect person-to-person before getting down to business. Relationships are very important to them.

Generates enthusiasm: They are "hip, hip hooray" people. They like lots of energy between and amongst people and for ideas and projects. They thrive on the "buzz."

Lives optimistically: They see the glass at least half full and even overflowing. They are "Can Do" people. When you look up "Silver Linings" in the dictionary, their face is next to the definition.

Acts impulsively: Their self-management is low. If an idea bursts on them, they will act on it immediately. They do not like detail and get impatient with too much information.

Easily distracted: Lots of things distract them from noises to visuals to smells. They can have a hard time focusing.

Dreams: They use their right creative brain more than their linear left-brain counterpart Thinkers.

Desires motivation: They can get bored easily and need to have activities and goals to inspire them.

Gets competitive: When push comes to shove, they can act more like Doers. That results in win-lose thinking and behavior.

Talker Expectations of You
- To be open, friendly, and enthusiastic.
- To share who you are and who you know.
- To get recognition and approval of their ideas, opinions, and beliefs.
- That action will take place immediately.

Talker—Sample Roles
- Sales
- Marketing
- Advertising
- Acting
- Radio/TV
- Call center

Summary

Negotiators in the Talker quadrant win about 24 percent of mutuality-based negotiations. Only 24 percent because when they get competitive, they become win-lose negotiators. Like Doers, they tend to be fast, tellers, I-centered, big picture, and poor listeners.

When negotiating with Talkers, you will need to pay special attention to managing discussions. They tend to be quite talkative and ramble and can take the discussions off track, moving to nonrelated subjects.

To negotiate successfully with Talkers, you should:

- Socialize a bit.
- Regularly recognize them and their contributions.
- Manage the conversation—keep them focused.
- Move fairly quickly.
- Make sure you know what they heard.
- Ramp up your energy level.
- Encourage their creative input.

Guardian—People-Oriented

Helps others: These are people with big hearts. They are often behind the scene, but being of service is one of their highest values.

Shows loyalty: Guardians are *people* people. They also make the best company person. They are loyal to others and loyal to the organization; sometimes to a fault.

Wants predictability: Guardians are not risk takers; they like to know what is coming. A predictable life is a safe life and they live for safety.

Keeps structure: They are very organized. Because they dislike anything that smacks of chaos, structure makes sense to them.

Avoids conflict: High Guardians avoid disagreement like the plague. They can find stern tone of voice, harsh words, and disagreeable ideas sources of conflict.

Appreciates precedence: As a form of predictability they like to know that an idea or practice has been used successfully by others before they will take it on.

Decides by consensus: Unlike their dominant opposites the Doers, Guardians feel most comfortable in checking in with others before making a decision. They want to collect opinions and ideas and go with the majority's vote.

Guardian Expectations of You

- That you will do what you say.
- That you will communicate in a supportive manner.
- That your relationship will continue long term.
- You will provide patient and thorough explanations.

Guardian—Sample Roles

- Administrative assistant
- Human resources
- Receptionist
- Police
- Bus driver
- Short order cook
- Customer service

Summary

Negotiators in the Guardian quadrant only win about 4 percent of mutuality-based negotiations; they so dislike conflict. And, conflict or disagreement is simply part of most negotiations. They tend to act more slowly, be easygoing and relationship-oriented, ask more questions, live we-centered and be somewhat better listeners.

When negotiating with Guardians, realize that they are much less willing to be openly honest with you until they fully trust you. So do not take everything on face value. They are a bit more guarded and will take more time before disclosing.

To negotiate successfully with Guardians, you should:

- Use warm tones of voice and pleasant language.
- Present new things safely and incrementally.
- Provide testimonials and assurances.
- Be highly supportive during and after the process.
- Structure your presentation well.
- Give them time to find consensus with others.

Working with Negotiating Styles Summary

When you become deeply knowledgeable about the four behavioral styles and master working *with* them, instead of disagreeing with or against them, everyone benefits.

Unfolding Case Study

Remember, the basic scenario is this. The timing is right to buy a side-by-side duplex as a rental property. You are actively searching. You will live in one side and use the income from the other apartment to help pay for the mortgage.

In addition to using your self-awareness and self-management, social awareness and managing relationships, relationships can be greatly enhanced when you bring behavior styles awareness into play.

Doer seller/negotiator: They will not care so much about you the person. The rental property is the "task" at hand. They are more apt to use the tactic "Take it or leave it" because they are self-confident that other buyers will show up to replace you. Because they tend to make up their own rules, they may not play fairly. They may tell you of other offers they have that do not really exist. They may inflate the house value because "playing fair" is not at the top of their value list. You need to do your own market research and be strong in your offers and sticking with your bottom line. They will "drive a hard bargain"; harder than any other behavior style. They also want the whole process to be shorter than long.

Thinker seller/negotiators: They are also business-first kinds of people. Schmoozing is not their strength. They will present lots of details and will want lots in return. They tend to be more rule oriented and will pay closer attention to the myriad details involved in selling a property. You will not be able to read as many visual or vocal clues to guide you. They tend to be more monofaced and monotoned; just the facts.

Talker sellers/negotiators: Plan on spending a lot more time with them. They are gregarious and want the time with you to be enjoyable on a personal level. They will be highly enthusiastic and attempt many ways of persuading you that this or that feature of the property has high worth and value. They do not care for details and that can be disastrous in a property deal. One thing leads to another and they may end up quite off track if you do not manage the conversations with them.

Guardian sellers/negotiators: Guardians are quite at home in homes. These structures represent safety and security to them. They will want the human factor to be present at all times during the exploration and negotiation. They do not like risk taking and may come across as very conservative and adverse to highly creative suggestions. They pay attention to details and that will help your process. Go easy on them and give them time to talk to others about whether the sale is a good one for them or not.

Questions to Ponder

- What is your dominant behavior style (BS)?
- What are your secondary behaviors?
- What are the strengths and weaknesses of each of your behaviors?
- What are the dominant behavior styles of your colleagues?
- What are the dominant BS within your family?
- What are the dominant BS of your friends?
- How can studying your colleagues, family, and friends help regarding negotiating partners?

Goals for Success

From the answers you get to the questions above, write S.M.A.R.T. goals that will lead to greater success dealing with varied behavior styles.

S.M.A.R.T. Goals for Behavior Styles Success

S. pecific

M. easurable

A. ctionable

R. elevant

T. ime Bound

I will _____

5

Integrating Six Principles of Ethical Influence

After covering the human fundamentals, emotional intelligence, and behavioral factors involved in negotiations, it makes sense to continue with the ingredients of influence and persuasion. These are part of the fabric of every negotiation (and remember, every conversation is a negotiation).

According to Merriam-Webster, "persuasion" is defined as "an opinion held with complete assurance." "Influence," on the other hand, is defined as: "the act or power of producing an effect without apparent exertion of force or direct exercise of command." I see these two working well together. In a negotiation, you know what you want to give and receive and sometimes have strong opinions on how that is to be achieved (unfortunately, that can be inflexible). So your job is to influence the other party into seeing or doing things as you want. Important to this book's model is that you do so ethically.

The fundamental concepts of ethical influence that we discuss in this chapter are based on the work of Robert Cialdini, PhD, from the University of Arizona. I add some complementary ideas, concepts, and practices to build on these foundations. Let us start with the basics of the Six Principles of Ethical Influence: Reciprocity, Liking, Social Proof, Authority,

Consistency, and Scarcity. We go through them one by one and then expand on each.

1. *Reciprocity:* People feel obligated to give something back to other people who have given them something.
2. *Liking:* People act more positively with others who they know and like.
3. *Social Proof:* People follow the lead of what other people are doing.
4. *Authority:* People rely on others who they perceive to have greater knowledge, rank or influence on how to act.
5. *Consistency:* When people take an action or make a commitment from their value base, they feel internal and external pressure to continue acting consistent with their initial commitment.
6. *Scarcity:* People put a higher value on that which they perceive to be less available.

Coming back to the concept that every conversation is a negotiation, you see that the six principles of (ethical) influence are present everywhere in life. The beauty of this application remains that the opportunity to learn about and practice the six principles are abundant. The more you practice these six principles, the better you get at using them. And the better you get at living and breathing the six principles on a daily basis, the more they will serve you in formal negotiations. Let us begin our discovery with "Reciprocity."

The Principle of Reciprocity

In its basic form, reciprocity is simply the give and take between and among people. There can be mental, emotional, physical, social, and even spiritual components.

Let us take a simple example of buying somebody lunch. We are talking here about an instance where the treating is not prearranged based on any prior conditions. It is one of those rather spontaneous, "Let me treat you to lunch today" occasions. Remembering that reciprocity is a two-way street, let us start with you first. I break this down to see if there are indeed any mental, emotional, physical, spiritual, or social aspects.

By mental we mean thoughts. Before any lunch-buying action takes place, you first have to have the thought that you would offer to pay for lunch. Even this simple thought did not occur in a vacuum. Who is this person to you? Do you like or dislike them? If you are thinking of buying lunch for someone you like, that thought usually comes from a place quite different than thinking about buying a meal for someone you do not like. You probably have an objective or motive to treat someone you do not like to lunch. You want to get something out of this. It is simply more agenda-driven than buying lunch because you like somebody.

The emotion we have been talking about here is "liking." Every mental thought we have is accompanied by an emotion. We are most often not aware of the emotions associated with our thoughts, but they are always there. Noticing the emotion is what we talked about in the EQ quadrant of self-awareness. A thought, or what is also called *synapsis*, creates a chemical in the brain. That chemical is now in the bloodstream and moves throughout the body. That is actually what we are talking about when we use the word *emotion* or *feeling*. So if you offer to buy lunch for someone you like, you have had a thought to do so that produced a chemical in your body that you translate as being a good feeling. Simple biochemistry. In contrast, if you have a thought to treat someone you *do not* like to a meal, the different chemistry produced will have a different feeling in your body. In some ways, the thought to buy lunch (what you might call a *positive thought*) is at odds with the feeling or emotion in your body that is one of dislike. Either way, reciprocity will be put into play. But will the return be positive or negative?

As you can see, the mental and emotional activities within you are now involving you physically. There is also the social nature to the two of you interacting around lunch. The spiritual side is this: What is the spirit of your gesture? What kind of energy are you in about the interaction? If you like the person, you will be of higher or lighter spirit. If you dislike the person, notice it or not, your spirit or energetic enthusiasm will be darker or lower.

This initial look into the mental, emotional, physical, social, and spiritual realms involved in reciprocity has been about *your* side of things. Let's take a look at the same situation from the *other* party's possible perspective.

Put yourself now into the point of view of the person (or people) who you are offering to treat to lunch. When they first hear your offer, they will have thoughts (*mental*). If you mutually like and respect each other (this will always be a matter of degree), their thoughts will more likely be positive. But even in good relationships this may not be the case. You have probably heard the expression, "giving is easier than receiving." In my experience, more people than not find this to be true. So what is up with so many people being uncomfortable on the receiving end of a gift?

What *emotions* the recipients of your offer have will depend on their thoughts about you. If they like you, their emotions will probably be positive. But even that is not a given. They may have issues about receiving that have nothing to do with you. People can establish a belief early on in their lives that they are undeserving. They have probably been told this by important people around them, and they take it in as their truth. This "personal" side of receiving may be reduced in professional negotiations. When being paid to negotiate, they may be able to objectify the process of giving and taking concessions. Still, it is hard to turn off all personal programing even with the best intentions. So as with all of the human factors, look underneath the professional veneer to see what personal characteristics might be bleeding through and affecting the interaction.

The *physical* side of reciprocity will be similar to your own. There will be tangible concessions involved along with the intangibles comprising the give and take of relationship.

Think of the *social* side of reciprocity from the other person's perspective. He or she is not your clone. So when it comes to giving and receiving, his or her personality will play a part. You will understand more of this as you integrate differing levels of emotional intelligence (in this case, social awareness and managing relationships) and also understanding varied behavioral styles. The general principle of reciprocity is still the base, but personal variations will influence the social factors.

The other party's *spiritual* or energetic state will also influence the give and take. Think about your own degrees of mood swings, positivity and negativity, your personal ups and downs. The other party has his or her own unique flows. You will have to pay attention to his or her state of being, or spirit, when determining what he or she might be ready to receive and how he or she might be inclined to give.

Gifts: In negotiations we call the tangibles *concessions*.

During your preparation you will have inventoried all of the tangible items from money to raw materials to end products that you can trade in negotiating. You will also have listed your organization's resources, skill-sets, and systems. The key to concessions is giving what is low cost to you and of high value to the other. Be proactive in offering the first concession or gift. This immediately sets the principle of reciprocity into play. The most powerful gifts are unexpected, meaningful, and customized. This applies to concessions.

Think about this as a receiver. You are in a negotiation session and have asked for delivery of a product no later than a week from Monday. The other party is thinking, "Mmm, we have the product in our warehouse, we have an efficient fleet of trucks, and we have room in our schedule; why not offer an earlier delivery date?" You, on the other hand, may not know that information. You may have been thinking of your more recent vendor with whom getting timely delivery was always a problem. Now this fresh offer comes in, delightfully beating your expectations of delivery time. They have offered you something that is of low cost to them and high value to you. Will your inclination be to clamp down on giving something back or being more receptive to returning their concession to you with one of your own? You can see that it can make sense to be the one who offers the first concession.

In trading tangible concessions and within the principle of reciprocity there is also a "Moment of Opportunity." If you make a request of the other party and they turn you down, they may on some level feel a little bad about their refusal. So the moment of opportunity is set up for you to immediately make another request. One way of setting up this opportunity is asking for something more than you expect they will give. After they say no, and you come back with a smaller request, the dynamic of contrast is now at work. They will be more inclined to say yes to your second request if they actually have the means to do so. So you can either purposefully set up the moment of opportunity (your own ethics are involved in doing or not doing this) or look for them as they emerge. The key is to always have a backup request.

The Principle of Liking

It is clear that human beings act more favorably to people they like. For instance, in selling (a cousin to negotiating), if all else is fairly equivalent, 70 percent of people will buy from those who they like. We want to find reasons to say yes to those we like and know.

There is a critical point to make right here . . . the key with this principle is *not* in getting them to like you first, but rather for you to find things to like about them. It is an automatic response for most humans to like people who like us. There is simply a nice flow of energy to this. If you think about this, it is actually easier to proactively look for things you like about another, rather than trying so hard to *get them* to like you.

What are the ingredients in liking somebody? The main three are: commonality, positive feedback, and cooperation.

Commonality: When you are with anyone, but particularly a fellow negotiator, proactively look for things similar between you. Similar backgrounds, experiences, attitudes, values . . . all have connecting points. As you see in the upcoming discovery phase, we suggest that you begin all negotiations (at least in person and by phone) conversationally. You will also see via negotiating styles or behavior styles that your conversations will be different with different styles. But the concept is the same. Explore things you have in common with the other. In two of my lengthy certification processes, as a health-care ombudsman and civil courts mediator, the first thing stressed was to find common ground between differing parties. Common ground binds us. And people who are joined, negotiators who are joined, are likely to have more successful negotiations.

For example, you are sitting down on the other side of the table with a new negotiator. You have done your preparation including research about this individual, and in looking at his LinkedIn profile you discover that you attended the same university. If you mention this common ground (and this person's university experience was a positive one), do you think he will feel closer to you or more distant? Closer is more likely. Again, the more common ground that you build at the beginning, the stronger your mutuality-based negotiating.

Positive feedback: What is it like for you when you get positive feedback from someone? Is your self-esteem higher or lower? Although behavior styles differ on how much positive feedback is acceptable, in general, people will feel better about themselves when they know they are seen in a positive light. Positive-feeling people/negotiators are more likely to negotiate positively. There is a three-leveled skill to learn here: praise, acknowledgment, and appreciation.

Praise: Praise is a high-level form of positive feedback. It is general and nonspecific—more of a good feeling kind of thing. Examples are "Well done!" or, "Nice job!" or, "Good idea!" These three and many more can also be used in a negotiation. You are giving almost no information, but the recipients will probably like what they are hearing. Therefore they will probably like you for giving the praise.

Acknowledgment: This is a more behavior-specific form of positive feedback. You will be telling the person what you saw or heard that you view as positive. Let us use the real estate buying situation. The selling party (fellow negotiator) has done a few things that you like. If you were to simply "praise" her, you might just say, "Thank you. That works." But remember, acknowledgment gets more specific. You might add these details: "The kinds of open-ended questions you asked really uncovered my preferences. The paraphrasing back to me showed that you listened deeply. And the way you organized in your summary of all of my different needs made everything so clear." Do you imagine the seller being angry or delighted with your specific feedback? It is more probable that she will like the feedback and therefore like you.

Appreciation: This is the least used but equally powerful member of the triad. Whereas acknowledgment gives detailed information about specific behaviors, appreciation is feedback about the character traits or values fueling behavior. What kind of positive character traits might you find in a fellow negotiator? Traits such as honesty, integrity, perseverance, and straightforwardness would be examples. So you deepen positive feedback to the seller, and building on the acknowledgment, you might say something like, "The number of questions and active listening you used showed that you really cared about me" (the quality is "caring"). "The tone of voice and words you used when you learned of the fire that has us looking for a new property showed your empathetic side" (the quality is "empathy"). "That really means a lot to me." Note: the chapter on negotiating styles or behavior styles helps you recognize that using appreciation will depend on the dominant behavior style of the negotiator. Some negotiators will very much welcome appreciation, whereas others will think it too earthy crunchy. You will have to use your emotional intelligence to determine when to use appreciation and to what degree.

Cooperation: This is the backbone of mutuality-based negotiating. Instead of naming this book *Negotiating Success*, it could have been titled *Cooperative Negotiating*. Working "with" the other party instead of "against" is the difference between a win-win and win-lose approach. I know that you know what it feels like when someone is competing against you versus cooperating with you. Nothing wrong with healthy competition, and that is likely to show up in sessions. The difference is intent and then actions. Competition to the death does not make for mutual gain. To the victor belong the spoils. But negotiating does not have to be going to war. A blend of competition and cooperation is best. You need all the skills in this book to lead a balanced approach.

The Principle of Social Proof

People sometimes use the phrase "herd mentality" when describing others. If you have watched a group of cows or a flock of birds, they often do the same things at the same time (there are always exceptions). One cow lies down and then eventually almost all will. One bird starts preening its feathers and soon the whole flock is doing that activity.

Humans can be the same way. In particular, people with a degree of Guardian behavior watch to see what others are doing before they feel comfortable enough to go along, too. An experiment I have tried many times is this: Stand at a street corner when the light is red (don't walk) when others are standing there, too. If no cars are coming (it is safe), cross the street.* See how many

---

*I am not advocating breaking the law. Know what the rules of the town are. In Singapore, for instance, just about nobody goes against the red because the police will readily fine you. In contrast, in Manhattan, New York, and downtown Montreal, Quebec, it is absolutely the norm to cross whenever there is an inch of access between cars.

people follow your example. Or, because there is often someone else who crosses first when they can safely move on to their next commitment, stand back and watch who follows this leader.

Take this analogy a little further. There are cultures and norms operating whether in cities like the above examples or within companies and industries. When people are used to following precedence, you can take a leadership role and set the new precedence, always for win-win results.

Let's come back to Guardians. People strong in this behavior style do not like to make decisions on their own. So they actually employ two aspects of social proof. If you want to offer a concession in a negotiation that is of good value to them but they are hesitant to try something new, cite other similar organizations (the more the merrier) who have successfully used your product or service. Testimonials and proof statements help high Guardians to feel safe. If others have agreed that there is benefit, they are more likely to also agree.

The second piece is about Guardians not liking to make decisions on their own. They check in with trusted others—social proof that it is okay to move forward. Expect to allow them extra time to confer with others. Be prepared to give them handouts and testimonials to share with others that what you suggest works. If you have time to allow time in a negotiation process, you may well come out ahead (as will they).

The Principle of Authority

What do we mean by authority? People rely more heavily on those they consider to have greater wisdom, knowledge, or status. Think about the many people in your life whom you consider authorities: parents, teachers, policemen, and older siblings (at first) bosses, governmental leaders, senior colleagues, even celebrities and sports figures as you mature. Our brains are deeply programmed to follow authority figures (that does not mean you have not pushed back against that learned behavior). Still, a good percentage of your negotiating partners will have predispositions to give a certain amount of credence to anyone they consider an authority. Knowing this, how do you use the information wisely for achieving mutuality-based negotiation results?

What can you do to have a leading edge (again, used ethically and wisely) for fellow negotiators to see you as an authority?

Credentials: In our Powerful Presentations training program, we teach participants to give strong and relevant credentials within the first 30 seconds of a presentation (and by the way, you are presenting in negotiations whether in person or by phone). Why? We want the audience (again, that can be one person or more across the table from you) to believe in you—to agree that you are an authority they can trust. Establishing yourself as an expert/authority increases receptivity in others. In negotiations, what serves you more: the other party being positional/oppositional/resistant or receptive? It just makes sense to be seen as a strong authority (not overbearing).

Clues: In addition to ensuring that your negotiating partner has factual information verifying your authority, how else can you solidify their perspective of you as such?

Clothes: What you wear can make a difference. Dress as a fellow negotiator would expect you to look as an authority on the topics you are discussing. Always wear clothes just a notch above the other (too much above and they cannot relate to you). Pressed and shined, look distinguished.

Title: Many companies use titles that do not necessarily convey authority. Check in on yours. Titles can be negotiable, too (with your boss, human resources, etc.). Look at yours through the lens of others (anticipated fellow negotiators). If it is strong, make it obvious before or at the start of the negotiation (even if you know each other, hand them your business card telling them that you want to ensure than they have your most up-to-date information).

Office: If you have the good fortune of negotiating in your own environment, make sure that all authentic signs of authority are visible: nameplate on your desk, certification plaques on your walls, neat and orderly appearance. Prearrange an intercom call with someone to tell them to hold your calls during the session. Get the drift?

If you are going to their office, understand that they might be pumping up their appearance of authority, too, and match them in strength-of-attitude.

When meeting on neutral ground, in addition to dressing smartly, ensure that you bring accessories that make your status apparent: unmarred briefcase, laptop case, handbag, and so on.

Body language: A strong (not stiff) upright posture, whether standing or seated, conveys authority. Be intentionally self-aware of what your face is conveying. We have some 240 muscles there that, according to Harvard Medical School, can make 7,000 faces. What message is yours sending? Uncertainty? Leadership? Other?

Tone of voice: Most people live unconsciously with their same-old voice day after day. Change that self-awareness; you can with practice! Your voice can convey authority, or lack of it; certainty, or lack of it; leadership, or lack of it. When your voice comes from your throat and nasal passages, you sound weaker. When you breathe diaphragmatically and bring your voice from your solar plexus, it has a deeper resonance. All of these changes make a difference that you can in fact control.

The bottom line is that, first, you have to know your stuff. That being a given, you can strengthen many aspects of yourself to portray the strongest you. Authority!

The Principle of Consistency

The idea here is that when people make a clear choice, clear to them and openly clear to others, they feel a certain pressure to stay with that choice. You might say that they now feel a personal pressure to defend themselves. In Reviewing Human Fundamentals (Chapter 2), we discussed the ego. Remember, the ego's main job is to keep us safe—to defend us. That is a strong force from within and one that you can count on being present in every single negotiator you ever meet. So once someone has stated a position about something overtly, the ego will defend that position.

Another way of talking about this is to say that when people declare a "value" of theirs, they want to be seen as consistently honoring that value. This is worth exploring here as it applies to you as well as your negotiating partners.

For the sake of this definition values are, first of all, intangible, not physical. They are the deeper qualities of life that bring us fulfillment when we have them present in our lives. The more we honor them, the happier we are. They can also be the guideposts that we look for when we notice that we are unhappy. When we notice less joy, we can ask ourselves, "What value is being stepped on or squashed here?" "What do I value that is not present?"

Values can also be equated with *needs*. You can ask, "What is the underlying need that I am attempting to satisfy now?" We often get lost in a strategy meant to have our values met and forget to look underneath that for the root need or value that wants fulfillment.

Do not confuse values with the *strategies* that you use to fulfill your values. Let's say that you value mobility. There are many strategies that will bring you mobility: walking, skating, hot air ballooning, pogo sticks, riding mowers, owning a car, living near a transit line, and so on. Given your current circumstances, you determine which strategies you can actually use that will help fulfill your value of mobility. Perhaps you cannot afford a hot air balloon right now. You may have a sprained ankle and cannot skate for a while. Your car may be in the shop and you need to find alternative transportation. Your value is still mobility and your job is to get creative with realistic options without getting stuck in any one method (see Chapter 8 on creativity).

Now let's throw in that you also value luxury. Then you may want to buy a Lexus or always travel first class, combining the two values.

But what happens when you get too attached to one way, one strategy only for getting your needs met? This happens all the time in negotiations. If one of your main values is mobility but you lose your job and so lose the Lexus, you may get very unhappy if you think that car is the only way to fulfill your value. A Ford will also get you where you are going (as will the bus). Remember, it is when we get positional (stuck) and reduce the field of possibilities that our unhappiness is usually what follows.

So with values being a little clearer, let's bring this back fully to negotiations. The sooner you get fellow negotiators to name what they value, the easier it will be to hold them to that. We recommend getting this started in the Discovery Phase when you are sitting down conversationally and getting the lay of each other's land, including their land of personal and professional values. Start with your own list. When I begin an important session (not negotiating a paperback book at a tag sale), I tell the other party how I will operate and request them to do the same. For instance, I name values of honesty, fairness, mutuality, integrity, and openness. Then I ask them if those values happen to be theirs, too. If yes, two things happen. We have just formed additional common ground and that helps when things get tough during the session(s). Then I ask if they are willing to treat me that way. If they say okay, great, you have a ground rule and commitment of consistency. Do write this down for all parties to see. That cements the commitment and will more deeply invite consistency later on. If no, you have an opportunity explore that. Do your best to understand their position. Perhaps they have never thought of these things nor had any practice in naming them. Unfamiliarity will often be a barrier at first. Gently work through that with education and encouragement.

Let's take honesty as an example. You have done all the preparation and discovery and are now trading concessions. Toward the end, they may declare that there is a "deadline" and that you must make a fast decision. You now have to determine if this is a tactic or not. There may in fact be a deadline imposed by others, with little or no wiggle room. It is then a fact and not a tactic (see Chapter 16 on tactics). If you discover that there is no real deadline but the other side made it up to pressure you to accede, you can now go back to values, the ground rule, and consistency. You call them on it and tell them of the consequences for being dishonest (you do this as diplomatically as possible so as not to trigger their powerful, defensive ego).

Most people do have scruples and do value being consistent with their openly stated values. Use this to everyone's advantage including your own.

Principle of Scarcity

When people (negotiators are people) perceive that what they want is in short supply, they place even more value on that service, product, or opportunity.

Recall all of the infomercials and other forms of sales (and we are constantly selling during negotiations) that warn "Limited Supply," or "Going Fast!" or "For the Next Three Days Only!" . . . all of these are calling on the notion that what you want is limited or scarce. It is intended to influence an emotional, knee-jerk response in you to give in and buy. Pressure! Is applying pressure ethical? Again, you decide what your own ethics are. You already know that there are many pressures within a negotiation. Whether they are real or just perceived is a sidebar conversation for another time. My view is that if you use pressure with genuine cause, then it is part of the process.

Preparation: During the first phase of negotiations, the Preparation Phase (again, more to come), be sure to give thought to all that you and your company have that may be in relatively short supply. Genuine scarcity! Another word that might be helpful is *unique*. What do you have that your co-negotiator needs or could use that no one else has? Or, no one else has it with the degree of expertise or quality that you and your company have. Going back to how the brain gets wired, it is most usual that when we deal with the same content every day (in this case, the resources, systems, skills, etc., we work with and around), our mind puts that into unconscious knowing. Picture that driving a car and all that you have to do during a ride is mostly accomplished without having to overtly "think" about it. But in preparing for a negotiation, it is the time to purposefully step back to re-inventory what you can offer in concessions (low cost to you; high value to them). And that is the perfect time to also make a sublist of everything that is unique, semi-unique, or just plain scarce. These items can be offered in a special presentation using the principle of legitimate scarcity to fuel increased appeal by the other side. How you frame it as such can make all the difference in how it is received.

Citing legitimate competition for your product, service, time, and so on, is also powerful. A recent example: A company I have been consulting with had some leading-edge technology. That means that its product was not only innately valuable but also in short supply—scarce. It doesn't take rocket science to know that if you have something unique, you might as well leverage that for your own benefit (the first win in win-win). There were two strong bidders for this new and benefit-laden product. One of the two bidders wanted exclusive rights to the product for three years (they were afraid their competition would gain market share). For the company I was serving, selling to only one customer would have been a win-lose proposition. Knowing that no other manufacturer could satisfy either customer's needs again highlighted the product's scarcity (probably short term as other manufacturers normally catch on in time). How could the selling company satisfy both customers without damaging relationships? The executive I was working with made it a point to discover what each of the two customers needed in addition to the product under discussion—things that my exec's company already had (low cost to them) but scarce within the two customers' systems (the second win in win-win). In this case, he created two win-win situations using double scarcity to satisfy (good enough) his customers.

The bottom line is that when you inventory your company's skill-sets, resources, and developed systems, some of them will be held in higher value by the other party because they are scarce to them. Use that scarcity to mutual advantage.

Integrating the Six Principles of Influence Summary

The six principles of ethical influence are reciprocity, liking, social proof, authority, consistency, and scarcity. Each of these areas has unique dynamics that can be used (ethically) when negotiating. In any given negotiation, there may be opportunity for more than one to be applied. Start to observe how these work in everyday life. Then start integrating them into your interactions with people. As always, the more you practice well, the better you will be at using from one to all of the principles in negotiations that matter to you.

Questions to Ponder
- What will you do to work on the give and take of reciprocity on a daily basis?
- What do you need to do to shift from wanting to be liked to finding things to like in others first?

- How can you use social proof to influence people for the good of both of you?
- What skills, experiences, knowledge sets, and personality traits do you already have that if properly portrayed, will have others see you as an authority?
- What can you do as a pilot program to invite people's values and then set up circumstances where they stick to those values?
- What inventory of benefit-laden things do you already have that few others possess (scarcity)?

Goals for Success

From the answers you get to the questions above, write S.M.A.R.T. goals that will lead to greater success of ethically using the Six Principles of Influence.

S.M.A.R.T. Goals for the Six Principles of Influence

S. pecific

M. easurable

A. ctionable

R. elevant

T. ime Bound

I will _____

6

Dissolving Conflict

Conflict! Disagreement! Dispute! Disharmony! Argument! Clash! The dictionary also lists "competition." Whatever the name, when you put two or more humans together, some degree of conflict will most likely arise. So, let us accept that it is so and then do our best to minimize conflict and therefore the potential negative results.

You have already begun to deepen your study and understanding of how to be a powerful conflict reducer through mutuality, proactivity and R.E.S.P.E.C.T., emotional intelligence, behavioral styles, and the six principles of ethical influence. Let us build on that for your negotiating relationship's success.

In Chapter 4 on negotiating styles, we talked about the original Golden Rule as "Do unto others as you would have them do unto you." Or, "Treat other people like you want to be treated." Following this adage is at least an intention of connecting with respect.

Even more positively influential though is the Platinum Rule: "Treat other people like *they* want to be treated." Why does that work even better? Think about yourself. If people knew how to treat you in ways that are aligned with your preferences and values, you would feel better. Feeling better minimizes conflict.

At this point, it is best to revisit a reality for most humans. We have an ego as part of our mind. So you probably do, too. The ego has an important job: it protects us. Unfortunately, the ego will go to great lengths to keep us safe, often at the expense of others. The ego is that part of you that blames, complains, and resents. It is the part that attacks and gets revenge.

On the other hand, the heart never attacks. No matter what you call it, operating from that place of your inner world known as *heart* will be much more peaceful. This is easy to say, but hard to do. The ego does not want to give power over to your heart. It is up to you to stay self-aware, feel and witness what voice is wanting to speak, and choosing heart over egoic mind when it comes to areas of disagreement.

Code of Conduct

This code of conduct is one tool that helps you to prepare in advance for all interactions with anyone and everyone you choose. That's a darn fine tool.

There are two basic ways of using this that we explore here—designed with others and designed with self.

Code of Conduct with Other

In this case, we frame the code of conduct with negotiations in mind. In the Discovery Phase, you can overtly call on the other party to join with you in an intention to be peaceful in the process. The operative word here is *be*. Most of us are trained heavily in *doing*. All too few of us are shown much about *beingness* (even though we call ourselves human *beings*). This is not earthy-crunchy, airy-fairy stuff (that would just be your ego labeling anyway). This is downright practical.

You can use whatever words work best for you in creating this code in your professional environment. Here, we use language that speaks directly to this process.

The simplest form of code of conduct is between two people. In this case, it is between you and a single other party. You two are different. Therefore, you two will have differences. And in negotiations, there are usually many things about which you may differ: personal style, goals, agenda, concessions, time frames, and so on. So there are many opportunities to disagree. This code of conduct is a way of being with others *no matter what* you are discussing. Isn't that cool!

No matter what subject you are discussing, the code of conduct question is: How do you want to "be" with each other about (name a subject)? So how do you want to be? Honest? Respectful? Open? Courageous? Caring? Empathetic? Understanding? Mutuality-based? The list is yours to fill in. Your values go here. And theirs. Together you build an agreed-on list.

Look, we know that many people will read the above and say, "I can't do that in a business setting." Or, "They will think I am nuts if I try this one."

And I say, be a leader. Try something new. Do not let Einstein look down from his heavenly perch and say, "There they go—disagreeing again. Will they never learn?" Stop the insanity. Why? It feels better! And when negotiators feel better about working with each other, the process is smoother as each gets more of what each wants. Each is also more inclined to support the other party getting what they want. Mutuality wins!

Here is a recent example. I met with a home builder out on a piece of rural land. Very nice guy! But his world is one of positioning, framing, and costs. He is not a human process–oriented man. When I arrived, he immediately began to walk the land and tell me where the house was going to go. No questions or inclusion of my ideas as customer. So I stopped him before things moved too far along (I knew that all of the things he was getting at would be part of our negotiations). I handed him a sheet of items I wanted to discuss about how we were going to proceed: a code of conduct between builder and buyer. I tailored what and how we discussed the list based on his behavior style. It went well. I trust that preliminary discussion about how we would work together will keep our relationship in good stead.

Now all the intending to "be" is well and good, but there is another human factor that must be dealt with. The physical brain has two nut-shaped components called the *amygdala*. This "middle brain" is the seat of our emotion. When we get triggered (angered you might say), the brain releases a hormone called *cortisol*. This response comes from the old "fight or flight" days and has served us well.

There is also a down side. Cortisol, produced by the amygdala when triggered, numbs our rational thought process in the frontal lobe (the seat of consciousness). Emotions take over. So when emotion is high, intelligence is low. Have you ever tried to make a clear decision when you were really ticked off? You simply cannot. The cortisol has to wash out of your system first. So the best thing we can do is to prevent the trigger (called an *amygdala hijack*) from happening at all.

So the code of conduct has a "do" part in addition to the "be" part. In fact, the do helps you back to who you want to be with the other. About anything.

What can you do? Well, what has worked for you so far in life to cool down, to get centered when you notice that you are starting to get a little frustrated, angry, or annoyed? Here are some things that might work for you:

- Breathe deeply for as long as it takes (usually five deep breaths at an absolute minimum).
- Stand up and move a bit.
- Stop looking at whoever you are triggered by (at least be aware that looking at them might be fueling your anger).

- Prepare in advance by having a favorite peaceful scene that you can bring forth and imagine being in right on the spot (a sunny beach, a mountain pasture, by a deep blue lake, etc.).
- Take a break.

You get the idea. Before you go and create a code of conduct with someone (and I am recommending you do this at the beginning of the Discovery Phase), make a list of anything and everything that you can do to cool down. When you regain control of your emotions, your intelligence rises and you can consciously return to how you want to be with the other in the session.

So when you are co-creating ground rules in the Discovery Phase, talk about how you are going to handle disagreements. Just the act of discussing an intention of harmony will help to produce it. Your code of conduct will go far in preparing each of you for the probable disagreements that lie ahead.

Code of Conduct with Self

You have a wonderful opportunity in knowing about *this code of conduct*. While it truly works to create with others, there may be barriers. They may not be willing. There may not be time. You may feel too awkward. But you can always create a code with yourself. In fact, I bet that you already have in your way.

Here is how it works. Take a look again at the process I outlined for creating with another. All of the ingredients are the same. Most often, how you want to be with one person will most likely be how you want to be with many others. With whom would you not want to be honest, respectful, open, courageous, caring, empathetic, understanding, mutuality-based? (Remember, the list is yours to complete.) When you create a code of conduct with yourself for how you want to be with people, you are creating a code for how you want to be in life. Every time, every place, with everyone, including within negotiations!

Conflict Escalation

If you are aware of how conflicts often escalate, you can watch for the signs and intervene early on. Six of the most frequent escalating steps are:

1. One or both sides' expectations are not met.
2. Sides look for ammunition.
3. People start attacking the other personally.
4. Threats are made.
5. Some try to punish the other.
6. Some involve others in their quest.

What can you do about this? Try to de-escalate the conflict.

Conflict De-Escalation

Examine motivations. Openly ask the others what their intentions are. Intentions are usually good but how we achieve them can be off track for the others. When you know people's intentions, you can speak about them and also brainstorm how to best achieve them (look to Chapter 8 for creative ways to do this). Here are six tips.

1. Listen. There is no better salve than being listened to.
2. Empathize. When people understand that you can relate to what is going on for them, they often calm very quickly (see Chapter 12, "Discovering All Sides").
3. Return to the "Why" (Chapter 10). Negotiations regularly get off track, and returning to your basic goals and reminding each other of the common ground works wonders to reduce tension.

4. Do something different. Whatever one or both of you have been doing has brought about the conflict. Stop doing that and try something else. (Caution—the ego loves power and struggle and will not want you to try something different. Find that heart center within you and do something different from that place.)

5. Take a break. Give that cortisol time to wash out of your body. Drinking a decent amount of water and moving around a bit will speed up the wash-out process.

6. Help the other save face. This is mutuality-based negotiating. You cannot have a full win-win if the other party feels bad in any way. Help them regain their natural mental and emotional health. Do what you can to boost their self-esteem.

Dissolving Conflict Summary

Conflict will arise. The best we can do is to be prepared in advance, catch the conflict early to reduce it, and return to more peaceful communication as quickly as possible for mutual negotiating benefit. Create a code of conduct, notice when a disagreement is escalating, and use the de-escalating steps to help make your negotiations more peaceful and productive.

Questions to Ponder
- What kinds of conflict do you get involved in?
- What triggers show themselves to you often enough for you to know what sets you off (annoys, aggravates, frustrates, etc.)?
- How do you currently react as part of the fuel of conflicts in your relationships?
- What will you do to expand the list of things to "do" to cool down and get more centered when you start to get triggered?

- When will you create a code of conduct with yourself and all others?
- With whom will you co-actively create a specific mutual code?

Goals for Success

From the answers you get to the questions above, write S.M.A.R.T. goals that will lead to greater success dissolving conflict.

S.M.A.R.T. Goals for Dissolving Conflict

S. pecific

M. easurable

A. ctionable

R. elevant

T. ime Bound

I will _____

7

Presenting Your Case

By now you are getting clear that the negotiations process is much more than just trading concessions. Although we spend plenty of time on the nonpeople nuts and bolts of bargaining later in this book, let us continue here with another important negotiation human dynamic: presenting your case. This chapter could have been included in either of the main two sections, The People in the Process or The Negotiating Process. It does contain steps and structure that fit well within the "process" of negotiating. But at the heart of Presenting Your Case are the intentions and skills involved in connecting and engaging human to human. These factors apply, whether you are in formal negotiations or not.

As you have learned in the material on emotional intelligence, people are giving off visual and vocal clues all the time. This includes you. So it makes sense for you to improve your knowledge and practice of presentation skills with two main objectives in mind. First, you can always improve your persuasiveness—the visual and vocal influence factors. How you present during a negotiating session will determine the strength or weakness of your influence. Your positive influence helps build rapport while your negative influence will foster conflict. Second, the more you build your presentation skills and self-awareness about how you are presenting, the more finely tuned your radar will be for how others are presenting back to you. All useful information.

We said at the beginning of this book that every conversation is a negotiation. And when you look at negotiating that way, you realize that you are practicing negotiating all the time. And whatever we practice well, we get better at. The same is true about presenting. Any time that you are seen or heard by another human being, you can consider that presenting. The material that is coming to you in this chapter is designed to be used in more formal presentations. This is a good match for you because the negotiation material in this book is really designed for formal negotiations (even though you will practice negotiation and presentation skills in all informal interactions, too).

Let's begin with some presentation basics.

Why People Buy

"Buyers?" you might say. In my view, we are always selling. Every conversation we have in life is, in effect, a sales call. I want my son to listen because I am selling an idea to him. I need for my wife to hear me so that my view gets heard (purchased). I want my boss to understand the suggestions and perspectives I offer in order to further my professional effectiveness. And I desire that the audiences of my presentations in negotiations take in what I offer (am selling) so that they act in a way that is beneficial to both of us.

To reach anyone's needs, we have to discover the W.I.I.F.M.—"What's In It For Me?" The W.I.I.F.M.s are the motivating factors within any human; the "why" or driving force behind people doing anything. If you look closely enough, you will discover that you always get something out of anything and everything that you do. I have worked with thousands of people on this subject. In every class around the world, a small percentage of people say that they get "nothing" from some things that they do. I welcome that as we then test that notion to see if it truly is their reality. This is important enough to explore here.

Recently a class participant pushed back, citing the following example: "I gave my brother-in-law a ride. I don't like my brother-in-law. I got nothing out of that interaction." Knowing that a value is always served when we take any action, I began asking questions. The background of my questions came from wondering whether he was getting something directly by his action or getting something he wanted by avoiding. After a series of questions, it became clear that he got at least two worthwhile things from giving his disliked in-law a ride. First, he did like his sister and got "appreciation" from her. Appreciation felt good to him as it is one of his values. He also values "service," and his act was one of service. He had done what many people do: he was stuck in the feeling of dislike and had not allowed himself to experience at least these two goodnesses that resulted. Until people make these connections, they will stay below the radar and not serve as fuel for motivation. It will help your job as a successful negotiator to understand these dynamics and perhaps overtly make the connections of reward for the other party, who may not have your knowledge on these things.

To continue then, in negotiations, there are two basic sets of W.I.I.F.M.: business needs and personal needs. We cover both in Chapter 11.

Image, Productivity, and/or Profitability

Three big-picture areas to explore are whether an audience member's primary need or area of importance (W.I.I.F.M.) is about image, productivity, and/or profitability. How will your support, information, service, or products help them excel in one, two, or three of these interest/buying areas?

Research each negotiating partner as much as you can in advance (again, Chapter 11). That helps you tailor how you slant your negotiation/presentation message and highlight how you will seek to find a win-win with their priority area in mind. We help you to engage them with Hooks in the 4 A's Setting Direction in a little while so that you are more on track and interesting to them.

Example: I recently taught our Negotiating Success experiential training program at BMW in England. If you think about this premier car company, you can probably relate to the nature of image, productivity, and profitability. Were you to negotiate with BMW, for instance, you would need to prepare in advance based on which area of the company your fellow negotiator worked in. For example:

- Who would be highly interested in "image"? The team members who spring to mind are car designers, marketing and sales professionals. Colors, sleekness, images to spark a buyer's imagination and preferences.
- Who devotes their work energies toward "productivity"? At BMW, fellow negotiators could be from the production line, gas consumption specialists, those who assess ease or difficulty of use for new software.
- Who are the professionals (at this car company) whose main focus is the financial bottom line: increasing income/profitability and decreasing expenses? CEO, CFO, purchasing, sales.

In summary, businesspeople will most likely have one or more of these three as the driving force behind their motivation for fulfilling goals that lead to their success. When you discover the other party's area of priority (beforehand, if possible, or during the second phase of negotiation, the Discovery Phase), you will be working with their W.I.I.F.M. factor. When you are in alignment with W.I.I.F.T. (What's In It For *Them*), you are on target to support achieving mutuality-based results.

Numb—Pain—Ready to Act

Another valuable series of steps is taking people from their indifference (*numb*) to their problems (*pain*) to a willingness to do something about their problems (*ready to act*).

Numb

Nobody is ready to act fully until they are more consciously thinking and feeling about their unmet goals and needs. Although you might think that your negotiating partner would already be in this state of awareness at any and all sessions, that may not be the case. Think about yourself as the human example. It certainly helps to be highly focused on what is immediately at hand (e.g., this hour of negotiating), but do you not have distractions? A text comes in at a break in the session and you have to shift your attention to that problem or situation. You are going through a divorce (or any other highly impactful life circumstance) that may take you away mentally/emotionally at times. Or perhaps you know that your boss is looking at this negotiation with a particularly watchful eye, and the stress of that comes over you now and then through your session. Research says that humans "go away" (think or feel about something other than the supposed topic or person at hand) 6 to 10 times per minute. Per minute! If your negotiation session is 30 minutes long, that is 180 to 300 times drifting away. You need to reengage them back to more full consciousness on your negotiation's topics. There are many, many reasons why it is important to actively engage your negotiating partners from the very start and to reengage them throughout the negotiations.

So, just because people are physically present does not guarantee that they are also mentally and emotionally engaged.

We use the term *numb* to warn you that they may not yet be hooked and ready to pay attention to you, your new idea, your service, or your product. Numb simply means that in a full and fast-paced world, people tend to take on not only what is in front of them but are juggling lots of varied priorities. I am sure you can relate.

An additional place to consider the other party's state of "numbness" is an opportunity you may uncover during your Preparation Phase or during the Discovery Phase. One of your jobs in negotiations is to unearth as many beneficial uses for your idea(s), product(s), and service(s) as possible by the other party. Though they will surely come to a session with their primary negotiation goals identified, like everyone else, they have blind spots that may be areas where your support and exploration will add benefit.

Three numb factors are worth considering in looking for extra opportunities over and above the negotiation's main focus:

1. Too busy—When we get too busy, lots of lesser priorities get pushed aside. They are still there and impacting business life but can get pushed under in the crunch. But the old adage is still true: "All you get for sweeping things under the carpet is a lumpy carpet." What lumps are your negotiating partners living with in the background that you might have some solutions for? It is worth probing for additional win-win results.

2. Tolerating—Another way of approaching numbness is to actively look for sore spots (pain spots). Human beings generally have a great capacity for tolerating (ignoring). This helps us get by in some ways but the sore spots still cause stress and at least partial failures. So the downside of tolerating is the upside for you in negotiations. What can you help bring back into the light that your negotiation partner has shelved (and those shelves are getting mighty overburdened)? Make it a habit to look for these opportunities—you will both come out ahead.

3. Low EQ—As we explored in Chapter 3, emotional intelligence is a great set of tools and awareness for greater success

in business and in life. Unfortunately, high EQ is still pretty rare. If your negotiating partner fits in the lower EQ group most humans are in, bringing your higher self-awareness, self-management, social awareness, and ability to manage relationships (in this case, negotiation relationships) to bear on behalf of shedding life on problematic numb areas may prove fruitful.

Pain

Pain refers to anything that is in the way of someone (or an organization) getting more of their full needs met. Unmet goals, marginal services/products, worry-points, failed expectations . . . are all pain points. Your job is not to create pain but to get others to reexperience the preexisting failures in the first moments that they are with you and your negotiation presentation. And the purpose of raising their pain points to a conscious level is not to be sadistic but to bring them to the point where they are *ready to act*, and ready to act in favor of your idea, service, product, and so on. You are being of mutually beneficial service and you hope that act of service gets them to consider your service/product with full attention.

When you craft your "Setting Direction Hooks" for the beginning of the Discovery Phase II (Chapter 12) with effectiveness, you are lifting your fellow negotiator from Numb to their Pain so they are Ready to Act for a win-win result.

Reception Challenges

All of the numb, pain, and ready-to-act ideas work much better when you have more complete attention from the other side. But human beings (you and your negotiating partners) have inherent barriers to the kind of communication that works best. It serves you well to take keep these in mind so that you make extra efforts in overcoming them. Let us explore them for further clarity.

- In general, people only hear about 50 percent of what is said.
  There are *lots* of internal and external "noises" in our busy, busy lives.

Internal (within each human)? We are complex creatures with 60,000 to 70,000 thoughts a day buzzing through our brain. Every time you have a chemical synapse called a *thought*, that sends a chemical signal to the body we call an *emotion* (remember, most people have low EQ). Each of those feelings is felt in the body (if one is aware of them, but for most people they go under the radar so they are subliminal noise). We have impulses and intuitions. Words from our left brain collide with images from our right brain. Our reptilian brain sends out old beliefs and memes unseen by our frontal lobe filtering system. Our brain processes some 20 million billion firings a second. Simply astounding!

External (environmental)? As many distracting noises as you can think of. Co-workers moving and talking, fluorescent lights buzzing, incoming emails "pinging," overhead fans swirling, a fire engine's siren wailing outside your window. And the distracting list goes on. Every one of them is a potential additional barrier to another human being (your negotiating partner) hearing important ideas, requests, product information, and so on, from you.

- Audience members only retain about 12.5 percent to 25 percent of your message.
  And this is only within 48 hours. The brain works in a "use it or lose it" way. If you have not made a strong impression as to why your idea, product, service, and so on, is *highly* meaningful to your negotiating partners, their

brain is less likely to retain what you have conveyed. This baseline poor retention rate does not serve you or your negotiating partners. Every presentation skill that you can use (and as offered in this book) will increase the likelihood that you will be a more persuasive negotiator. Note-taking is helpful. Aside from being something you both can refer back to, the kinesthetic act of writing helps the brain lock on to the information.

- Humans mentally "go away" about 6 to 10 times every minute.

    This is a slightly different way of understanding that people only hear 50 percent, on average. This is true particularly through less interesting times in the negotiations. It is a reminder that you constantly have to Rehook/Reengage them; make it interesting. You speak at about 165 words per minute, whereas the listeners think at about 800 words per minute. That is a lot of time for them to be placing attention elsewhere. But every time they (or you) go away, essential information may get lost. This can lead to misunderstanding and conflict. There is no "perfect" here, but you can improve the odds of higher intake and retention by presenting your ideas and arguments in more compelling fashion.

Having explored some of the foundations of receptivity in others receiving our information, let us return to behavior styles. We build on Chapter 4's more extensive study of behavior (negotiating) styles by first looking from your side as the presenter of information.

Doer as Presenter

If you took the time to go through the initial behavior styles material in Chapter 4 (check marks next to the behaviors that you exhibit frequently), then you can make better use of the following material.

Whenever you are being seen and heard, you are presenting. Because we all have strengths and weaknesses with regard to our varied behavior styles, studying the following effective and ineffective behavior as a presenter of information allows you to make changes that serve the mutuality-based negotiation process.

If you tend to have a good deal of Doer behavior in you, your areas of *effectiveness* in presenting your argument may be that you are:

- Impromptu
- Decisive
- Big picture
- At ease
- Owning the room

Let us break these down:

- *Impromptu:* You have a strong ability to make things up on the spot. You can engage situationally in what your fellow negotiator brings to the table.
- *Decisive:* Being a strong decision maker in negotiations is a fine strength. But remember, every strength can be a weakness. The rap on high Doers is that they negotiate in an "it's my way or the highway"—too decisive, too quick, and too strong.
- *Big picture:* Not everybody can paint a clear overview or summarize complex material well. Doers with this ability can add lots of value to detailed negotiations.
- *At ease:* Surprises? They do not rattle you. You can go with the flow. People who get nervous in negotiations tend to concede more concessions than they need to.
- *Owning the room:* If you are a typical Doer, you have a very strong personality. That can be a positive or negative

character trait based on what behavior type your fellow negotiators are. If your attitude and intention is to use your strength of character to ensure win-win results, then you are well ahead of most Doers.

If you tend to have a good deal of Doer behavior in you, your areas of *ineffectiveness* in presenting your argument may be that you are:

- Bottom-line driven
- Aggressive
- Poorly structured
- Impatient
- Big picture only

Again, let us break these down for further clarification:

- *Bottom-line driven:* You probably do not like details. Unfortunately, negotiations are filled with details. High Doers prefer to get straight to the point. Well, that works with other Doers, but Thinkers and Guardians need more detail. And Talkers and Guardians need more of the human touch before they are ready and willing to proceed with the business at hand.
- *Aggressive:* This is a subjective response to strong behavior. Still, 50 percent or more of people report finding people with high Doer behavior to be aggressive in their eyes. And that is not a positive for them. Short, to-the-point sentences appear too abrupt to these people. They take a clipped, monotone delivery as being too sharp. Lack of warmth in your face has them recoil for lack of human connection. That surely does not serve mutuality-based relationships.
- *Poorly structured:* For many of you, taking the time to ensure well-developed, detailed-oriented and linear communication

is not a priority. But for Thinkers and Guardians, it is imperative to include these for their easy digestion of information.

- *Impatient:* You typically like things to be presented in the big picture (you grasp things so quickly), and the fewer the questions the better. But 50 percent of people (classified as Thinkers and Guardians) need that extra time and detail to make sense of your statements, ideas, and arguments. Your impatience with their needing more time to think things through (and Guardians need more time to consult with others as they make decisions by consensus) puts them off. That gap-making does not foster win-win results.

- *Big picture only:* While this was also listed as an effective trait, if you cannot go to the detail for those who need that for understanding, this has turned into a negative. Understand that about 50 percent of people are simply not as fast as you in grasping things. Discover how much more detail they need and do your best to provide it. What they understand can absolutely help you in getting what you want, too.

Caution: Doers have the second-lowest success rate in win-win negotiations. Why? They drive too hard. An attitude of "What's mine is mine and what's yours is negotiable" does not sit well with your negotiating partners.

Thinker as Presenter

If you tend to have a good deal of Thinker behavior in you, your areas of *effectiveness* in presenting your argument may be that you have:

- Good structure
- Strong detail

- Linear presentation
- Audience inclusiveness

We will break these down for further clarity:

- *Good structure:* Tying things together in a linear fashion probably comes naturally to you. Other Thinkers along with Guardians will appreciate your delivering information in a way that they are used to themselves. It also helps Talkers make sense of things as they tend to be much less capable of organizing their thoughts like you do.
- *Strong detail:* You most likely see things in all their complexity. You have a solid ability to draw the entire picture for greater clarity of all that is involved.
- *Linear presentation:* Bouncing around simply confuses people. Your fellow negotiators will more likely follow the progression of ideas about how your product or service will work for them when you deliver the information in logical fashion.
- *Audience inclusiveness:* You are more likely to take others into account when you are on a topic. Unlike more highly independent negotiators (Doers and Thinkers), you think about how all the ingredients (including the people) fit together for greater success. That binds people instead of separating them.

If you tend to have a good deal of Thinker behavior in you, your areas of *ineffectiveness* in presenting your argument may be that you are:

- Too detailed
- Monotoned
- Low animated

Again, let us look into these more closely:

- *Too detailed:* While all that detail helps you to make sense of things, Doers and Talkers are used to working with the bigger picture and may get bored with you and what they consider unnecessary information. If you know that additional information is critical for your fellow negotiators to have for the best decision, find means of getting it to them in ways that they can accept. Handouts and follow-up email attachments may be better timing for them. And cut down on your normal desire to give lots of detail as a good practice for your versatility, too.

- *Monotoned:* You may ask, "Who cares about tone of voice? The facts are what matter." Again, this may be the way you see the world, but at least 50 percent of people want more of a human connection before they are ready to deal with "facts." Warm tones connect for them. And more pitch (modulation, inflection) makes things more interesting in their experience. That interest will certainly help you get more of what you want in a negotiation. Very practical this!

- *Low animated:* Again, you may be saying: "What does having more facial expressions or using hand, arm, and head gestures have to do with the facts? It is not about the facts but how people take the facts in." Many fellow negotiators will depend on what they see as they watch you for clues as to how interested or even trustworthy you are. If you have the traditional poker face, they cannot read anything but words. Words by themselves are lacking all of the other visual and vocal clues that are part of good communication.

Caution: Although Thinkers are the most successful win-win negotiators (great structure, think issues through, strive for "we win" results), they also expect others to play fairly (which many people have not been trained to do). So they often give away too many concessions, expecting a quid pro quo that does not materialize.

Talker as Presenter

If you tend to have a good deal of Talker behavior in you, your areas of *effectiveness* in presenting your argument may be that you are:

- Energetic
- Impromptu
- Inspirational
- Optimistic
- Expressive

Let us look into these for further clarification:

Energetic: You probably have a gregarious and bubblier personality than most. That enthusiasm will serve you well when explaining or demonstrating your idea, product, or service.

Impromptu: Like Doers, you have a strong ability to make things up on the spot. You have a creative streak using the images and intuitions supplied by your right brain. This can be a powerful ingredient when negotiations get stuck.

Inspirational: You lift people up. Many negotiations get mired down in minutiae, but you are able to show fellow negotiators how to get back onto a positive track.

Optimistic: Again, negotiations can go sour in the details. You see the glass as half full or even overflowing. Abundance versus lack is a powerful tool when seeking mutuality-based outcomes.

Expressive: It is easier for you to relate what you want and need than many. Your vocal tones and facial expressions are important in communicating; with honing, you can bring these pluses to serve both parties well.

If you tend to have a good deal of Talker behavior in you, your areas of *ineffectiveness* in presenting your argument may be that you:

- Ramble
- Get lost
- Act impulsively
- Only share big picture

We dig into these further:

Ramble: For you, talking is easy. And talking and talking and. . . . The acronym W.A.I.T. can serve you—"Why Am I Talking?" Listen more and the other party will appreciate you more. You will also receive lots of good information to aid you in the session.

Get lost: One thing leads to another for you. It is true that everything is interconnected but if you get three or more degrees away from the agenda item you are discussing, it gets confusing or irrelevant to the topic at hand. Staying focused and on target has lots of value. You get to explore a specific topic more deeply with agreement about actions more probable. This takes emotional intelligence's self-awareness (of when you are getting off track) and self-management (to bring yourself back on target). This also reduces or eliminates the frustration the other party may be feeling about your getting lost.

Act impulsively: It is often said about high Talkers that anything shiny draws their attention away. The shiny can be a thought, sound, thing. . . . Without self-awareness about this going on and self-management to not act (impulsively) on the incoming stimuli, you may allow yourself (and your partner) to be pulled into unproductive territory. This sabotages time management and can dismantle a solid negotiating relationship.

Only share big picture: You have this in common with Doers. Unfortunately, Thinkers and Guardians rely on lots of detail to make sense of everything. They need to know how things work before deciding on their value. With practice, you can start any new habit you want to (says neuroplasticity). Begin adding a little more detail in your everyday life and you will be better able to do this in negotiations, too.

Caution: Talkers are the second best at achieving win-win results. But they are quite behind the number one Thinkers. Sociability, optimism, and enthusiasm are powerful positive allies in sessions. But rambling and impulsiveness are negatives. And when Talkers get pushed (as is bound to happen in negotiations), they get competitive. Competitiveness can absolutely result in win-lose results.

Guardian as Presenter

If you tend to have a good deal of Guardian behavior in you, your areas of *effectiveness* in presenting your argument may be that you:

- Create good structure
- Inspire harmony
- Calm people

Let us unpack these for additional clarity:

Create good structure: Successful negotiations need good structure because in the end, it is attention to detail that produces the satisfaction level in the short and long term. Your contributing good structure also helps keep the fast-paced Doers and more scattered Talkers within the negotiation ballpark.

Inspire harmony: The nature of negotiations is to have differences to iron out (otherwise you could just sign the deal because everyone is already in agreement with no need to "negotiate"). So do bring your desire and ability to create harmony to the table.

Calm people: As the warmest people of them all, you have the ability to ease tension on others. Warm tones of voice and understanding facial expressions go a long way to calm the charged-up egos of the others. But you can get even better at calming people by doing so proactively. You will need to call on the Doer in you to be more actively calming.

Caution: Guardians are the least successful win-win negotiators because they so dislike conflict—lack of harmony—that they avoid strong discussion and cave in rather than feel inharmonious feelings.

If you tend to have a good deal of Guardian behavior in you, your areas of *ineffectiveness* in presenting your argument may be that you have:

- Low energy
- Few gestures
- Low projection
- Poor time management

Let us explore these aspects a bit further:

Low energy: You typically like to do things behind the scenes. You are not a show-off. But the daily habit of being this way has programmed your brain to express less overtly. Negotiations often demand a strong presence when emotions (or energies) do run high. What will it take for you to get more energetic for more positive results?

Few gestures: Low expression means lower communication. It also indicates lack of enthusiasm. Doers and Talkers take advantage of this as they are stronger personalities who can easily dominate you. If they are reading the nonverbal clues you give off by a static (lack of gestures) presentation of ideas, and so on, you are already behind in the game.

Low projection: This is about projecting your voice, the volume. As an easygoing person, you likely have a soft voice. But negotiations are not a time to be soft. A strong voice (higher projection) gives the message that you believe in your idea, product, service . . . strongly. And that your goods have high value. Weak voice weakens your argument, whereas a strong voice strengthens your presentation.

Summary of Behavior Styles as Presenters

Every human has behaviors. Our behaviors are strengths and weaknesses based on who we are with and what our objectives are. Knowing your own practiced habits, tendencies, and therefore preferences is a good starting point for then relating to others who have their own unique blend of behaviors.

In presenting our thoughts to other parties in negotiations, all of these behaviors could potentially come into play. When our behaviors are compatible with others, there is reduced friction and misunderstanding and greater degrees of effectiveness in the process. The good news is that you are the one who has practiced whatever behaviors you have today, and over time, you can change your behaviors to bring you greater success. It takes study, time, and commitment. But when you clearly define the W.I.I.F.M. to do so, you will have the motivation to persevere because changing habits (changing the wiring and firing of your neurons, dendrites, etc.) has a degree of discomfort and challenge involved. But as a colleague of mine likes to say, "Success is the only option!"

Setting Direction—4 A's

After you have done your preparation for an upcoming negotiation session (Chapter 11), it is time to meet (and again, in-person meetings are simply more powerful when you can). The opening moments of the meeting are critical. They set the tone and gauge interest and receptivity. The 4 A's Setting Direction opening is a wonderful tool to get things going for an amicable, organized, and mutuality-based productive session. The "audience" is your fellow negotiator(s). You can use the form below to map out your opening.

A—Audience Hook

Let us start with the Audience Hook. Remember to start with the working assumption that while your negotiation partners are physically in the room, they are *numb*. Just before your session begins, they may be working on their BlackBerrys. Maybe they had a fight with their spouses and they are still emotionally charged. Perhaps they have reports due this afternoon and are mentally preoccupied. You have got to get them mentally and emotionally back into the room with you. How will you do that? By using Engagement Devices.

An engagement device is just what it says; your aim is to deeply engage the other party on topic. You can open the session's conversation in a number of ways:

- Questions (to be answered)
- Rhetorical questions (to be answered internally)
- Stories
- Quotes
- Statistics
- Examples
- Testimonials

- Comparisons
- Jokes/humor

Let's go through each briefly so you have a better sense of why to choose one over the other for your goals in any given session. Please give strong consideration to the behavior style of the other party. Last, we use the sample negotiation case of sitting down to iron out the purchase of a rentable property.

Questions: All behavior styles respond to questions. The Engagement Device that is most universally suited to engage all behavioral styles is the question (to be answered for discussion). A powerful question is designed to have each and every negotiating partner (over time) think and feel about the answer in their own situations, their own life. Asking a question puts you somewhat in control as the director of the topic.

Adding to that dynamic, using negative-based questions is designed to get people out of numb by immediately going to the problem that currently exists. This is whatever the other party needs from you that they do not have (otherwise they would not need to negotiate anything).

Another guideline about hooks is to *always use at least two engagement devices*. Why? First, people may be preoccupied in the ways mentioned earlier so they may not even hear the first question. And second, the second question will allow you to deepen the *pain* individually for every audience member.

Rental property example: After saying hello (and remember, each of the four behavior styles has different preferences on how that happens), you could start off the Discovery Phase conversation with something like, "How has the poor housing market affected your wallet?" Your next questions could be, "If this property doesn't sell quickly, how might that make matters even worse for you?"

See, this kind of questioning primes the pump for greater receptivity to your offer. Make sense?

Rhetorical question: Everyone responds internally to rhetorical questions. "Hello . . . the housing market has been awful lately and I am sure that's affected your income right? If this trend continues, will your business suffer even more?"

Story: Talkers love a good story. Tell any story (can be considered a Proof Statement and the more local the better) that sets a positive view of working with buyers like you.

Quote: Doers appreciate a quote from someone they admire. For example, search the web for a quote that will drive home the point of selling to someone you like. I just put this into a search: "quote about people buying from people they like" and among the responses was, "People buy from people they trust and they trust people they like."—Garrison Wynn. So using something like this could be the message about having a civil and conversational session. You can also then ask a follow-up question.

Statistics: Thinkers love statistics. You might say, "Did you know that 73 percent of rental properties sell within the first 50 days if the price is just below market value? How long have you been holding on to this property?"

Example: All behavior styles can respond to examples. You could ask a risk-based question and follow with an example/statistic such as, "What would it be like for you if you didn't sell this property in the next six months? For example, in nearby Harrow County, 81 percent of properties that did not sell in the first half a year actually took 1½ years to sell."

Testimonials: Guardians feel much safer when others have successfully tried something before. The conversation might begin, "Have you ever been burned at closing after going through a lengthy process with a prospect? I have three banks willing to vouch for the solidity of my financials."

Comparisons: This can work well with all behavior styles. Perhaps you say, "If you compare sales in the early winter with sales in the late spring, you will know how dead the market is now. Still, I would like to explore how to turn that around between us."

Jokes/humor: In general, I do not recommend starting off with a joke. Negotiations should be congenial, but they are usually serious enough not to start too lightly. Talkers like a good joke, but that can get them thinking of other jokes to tell you back and get everything a little off target right away. In my experience, appropriate humor can break tension if sprinkled throughout the session. But you've got to know your audience and their style. You can be light at the start of a negotiation but if you want to hook the other party using their unmet needs, goals, concerns, problems etc., leave the humor for a little further in.

In summary, use an engagement device to get your negotiating partners more in touch with their topic "pain" from the very beginning of your negotiation (Discovery Phase). This will have them more receptive to what you have to offer in concessions to eliminate their pain.

A—Answer

Let us talk about the second A. Now that you have used the Engagement Devices to get them to live their *pain* in the here and now, it is time to indicate that what you bring to the table will bring them solutions to those problems.

Take a look at the form and the second A: "Answer and Presentation Title." If you were to advertise your negotiation solutions as a presentation, what would the title of it be? Using the real estate example above, your title might be "A Successful Deal for 456 Union Street." Write the title of a real-life negotiation topic you have on the form below.

You will use this title in a single sentence that tells them what topic you are going to cover and loops back to the previous problems uncovered. After you have opened with your engagement devices/hooks, you could say, "So today, let's work together to have a successful deal regarding this property."

Next, you can use a bridging, or transition, sentence. Once again, I refer to Dr. Cialdini. In his research, he discovered that when you give people the "reason why," 83 percent of people are more apt to go along with you. You might call this the *because* factor. There are two phrases that work well to tell the audience why you want them to pay attention to the upcoming three agenda items. They are: "So that . . . " and "In order to . . . ".

For example, you could say, "So that we have the most productive conversation about the property, I suggest that we cover these three agenda items . . . " and that leads you right into the third A: "Agenda."

A—Agenda

For some reason, people remember things grouped in threes. One, two, three; A, B, C; Do, Re, Me; people die in threes. . . . So we suggest that you keep the number of agenda items to three. When you actually bargain, you will discuss lots of points and subpoints. But you are just giving them the big picture now—telling them where you want to go.

Think of your suggested agenda items as titles only. Three or four words, tops. This makes it punchy, more memorable, than a narrative sentence. You are simply telling them what you think you are going to discuss at length in a little while. Your three agenda items for the property at 456 Union Street might be:

1. Items that need to be fixed in the building.
2. Nonmonetary aspects of the deal.
3. Time frame for closing.

A—Audience Takeaway or Action Plan

Even though you are just into your conversation for a minute and a half, it is time to set the expectation for your negotiating partners about what they could take away from their time with you. This is meant to fill their W.I.I.F.M. so that they stay engaged with what you have to offer.

You could say, "By the end of this meeting, if we approach this deal in right attitude, I trust we can reach a mutually agreeable settlement."

The worksheets below can be your guide for many conversations/presentations/negotiations to come.

Setting Direction Worksheet

The 4 A's

Audience Hook—W.I.I.F.M. (or, from your vantage point, What's In It for Them?)

What does your negotiating partner need (from you)?

_____

_____

Engagement Devices/Hooks (at least two) _____

_____

_____

_____

_____

Answer (to Their Need)

Presentation Title _____

_____

"Today I suggest we discuss _____

_____

_____ "

Bridging Sentence ("So that . . . " or "In order to . . . ")

_____

_____

_____

Agenda:

1. _____

2. _____

3. _____

Audience Takeaway/Action Request:

"By the end of this session, we will (have . . . , be able to . . .)"

_____

_____

_____

_____

Summary of Behavioral Styles 4 A's Satisfaction Points

Doer: Is interested in all four aspects of the 4 A's.

Talker: Will have particular interest in the Audience Hook, Answer, and Action Request.

Thinker: Is interested in the entire 4 A's opening, but particularly the Agenda.

Guardian: Will stay tuned for the Answer, every detail of the Agenda, and be interested in the Action Request.

Using Your Voice—The 6 P's

Dr. Albert Mehrabian, professor emeritus of psychology at, UCLA, has become known best by his publications on the importance of verbal and nonverbal messages. His studies found that people trusted or believed what a speaker was saying based on the visual, vocal, and verbal composition. I have rounded his numbers for ease of remembering. The awareness of these factors is what counts. His actual numbers were 55 percent visual, 38 percent vocal, 7 percent verbal.

Visual	60%
Vocal	30%
Verbal	10%
Total	100%

Most negotiators never give a single moment of thought to how their voice influences the negotiations process (another reason to *not* negotiate solely by email). But as shown above, when you are bargaining in person, your fellow negotiator is unconsciously placing about 30 percent of their believing you on how you sound to them. When you negotiate by *phone* with no visual clues to rely on, each of you will depend on the other's voice for 70 percent of the believability and trust of each other. Those are powerful numbers and not to be taken lightly.

So what can you do to make a more powerful (and positive) influence on the proceedings? There are four basic mechanical ways to use your voice for more interest and persuasion: pitch, pace, pause, and projection. Let us take a quick look at the basics of each.

Pitch: The ups and downs of your notes. Monotone bores people. A bored fellow negotiator will be less excited about what you have to offer in return for whatever they are willing to give. Pitch indicates interest. You have to appear to be interested in what you are offering. It also helps to be perceived as interesting. All are accomplished by appropriate variety of modulation, intonation, or pitch.

Pace: The speed at which you talk. Monopace is also boring. But the ground rule is that if you regularly talk too fast, the other party will have to work too hard to keep up with you. Negotiations are already a lot of work. Do not add this as an extra barrier.

You can speed up your pace to create a sense of excitement or slow it down for emphasis. Speeding up can also be used to de-emphasize. A good contrast practice is to speed up when you admit to not being able to offer something. But slow the words or phrase down when you want something you offer to appear significant. If you were to use this methodology in the real estate example, it could sound like, "I am sorry that I cannot come up with the money in seven days [speed up " . . . cannot come up with the money in seven days"], but what I *can do* is to *guarantee* that the *bank will approve* the loan when my present home sells." You would sloooow down the words and phrases *can do*, *guarantee*, and *bank will approve*, making them seem quite solid in contrast to what you cannot make happen.

Pause: Stop for a moment for effect. Many negotiations have lots of little moments of significance. Pause before or after a significant point, for emphasis. Pausing also helps to slow down a nervous fast pace. Let us use the exact same sentence we used in Pace in the real estate conversation. You have emphasized *can do*, *guarantee*, and *bank will approve* by drawing those words out a bit. All you need to do to drive the point home is to add even a nanosecond pause after " . . . but what I can do . . . " to set up a little psychological anticipation. You can minipause between *bank* and *will approve* and again just after *guarantee*. Consciously and expertly sprinkle pauses throughout your session to add a solid degree of persuasion. And to become expert at anything, you will need lots of practice.

Projection: How close or far our voice can be heard; how loud or soft. Why vary your projection? Mono anything is boring for the other. And boring has no influence but in the negative. In general, I suggest that you come on stronger than weaker in any negotiation session. But, as we saw in studying varied behavior styles, there are degrees of everything, including strength. The idea with projection is to get in and stay in conscious touch with how strong or weak your voice is sounding. Too weak and Doer negotiation partners will dive in for the kill. Too strong and

Thinkers and Guardians will withdraw. Delivering the degrees of vocal strength is indeed an art that takes lots of practice. But the positive outcomes will be tangible.

Remember that when you are negotiating via phone, 70 percent of your influence comes via your vocals. While changing your projection is a bit tricky over the airwaves, you can clearly vary your pitch, pace, and pause to improved effect. You will not always use the adage to "put a smile in your voice." There are plenty of times in a telephone-based negotiation to make points with a sterner, more concerned voice of objection. But do consider the phrase as a reminder to pay attention to your vocals. A year or so ago, I remembered how advantageous it is to have a mirror on one's desk, and so I put one there. What an ally. Our faces and voices work in sync with each other. Checking in on your mirrored expressions will help you stay in touch with how your voice is coming across. You then adjust according to your ever-changing negotiating purposes.

Passion: I consider this the fifth P—the fuel that drives the four physical or mechanical Ps. This is the color, warmth, and meaning given to your voice. These qualities are what tell your fellow negotiators that you love what you do and are very happy for the opportunity to share your information with them. Adding emotion to your voice will give it color and warmth with a strong positive influence. (By the way—as an old career counselor, I must say that if you do not have a solid degree of passion for the work you do and therefore the ideas, products, and services you negotiate, start looking for other work. Life is too short to spend time doing what you do not enjoy.)

Practicing: Your brain wires and fires in repeated fashion. But if you keep on doing what you have always done, you will keep on getting what you have always got. Not good enough for becoming a premier negotiator. Have fun with your voice. Not only will your persuasion become ever better by adding appropriate vocals at just the right times, but you can also add a bit of fun to your life through practicing vocals. Anytime you talk, you can consciously practice your pitch, pace, pause, and projection.

- *Reminders:* When I first started learning that I could have more positive effect with appropriately varied vocals, I put a small yellow sticky-note on the wall next to that old phone. It simply read "4 Ps." Every time I picked up the phone to answer or call out, I was reminded to play with my tones. Think of a reminder that will work for you.

- *Smartphone:* Most phones have a feature for recording your voice (I use it for memos to self, writing songs, practicing my vocals). Play with whatever P is your weakness. Have others listen to the before and after of your practice sessions.

- *Children:* Children are not excited by monotone reading. They are wonderful people to practice with by using your expanded ranges for greater interest and persuasion. If you told a four-year-old that "the mean old wolf was going to eat the little girl" using monotone, do you think they would truly believe you? Neither will your negotiating partners.

- *Foreign accent:* There are a zillion accents on this amazing planet. Some years ago, I realized I was still using the rather fast and flat New York voice I grew up with. When my wife and I went to Ireland on vacation, I decided to try to sound like those fair people. With quite a lot of practice, my brain and voice started to get the hang of the Irish lilt. And then I realized that as my brain took that on for playfulness, my regular speech was becoming more pitch-laden and interesting.

- What accent grabs your attention when you hear it? This is not about being a great accent producer (I was told mine "sucks" by a man from Northern Ireland). The practice is for fun and improved vocals. Play with your preferred accent whenever it feels safe enough for you. As an aid, you can also get web downloads or CDs by speech coaches (often designed for actors mastering an accent). Anything you do along these lines will help you get in touch with your voice in ways that will indeed add a depth to your negotiations rarely thought of by anyone. Another edge for you!

- *Radio scripts:* I have included an exercise next that we use in our Powerful Presentations and Executive Presentations training classes. You can practice in the privacy of your own office or home at your leisure. The idea is to pretend that you are interviewing for a job as a radio announcer. Recording these scripts while you read them in various ways will be a clear gauge of how you are doing. Again, let a close friend or colleague listen, too, as their brain is free of your own brain's unconscious vocal programming for a more neutral take.

Radio Audition Script

How would you like to be an announcer for radio or television? What do you need to do to be hired into that position? How do you need to sound to beat out the competition for the job? (Sometimes you *are* competing in negotiations for the deal.)

1. **Confidential and intimate:** A good announcer (negotiator) must wear many vocal hats. Sometimes she or he needs to sound confidential and intimate:

    "Friends, if you are like so many lonely people—and I think you are—you have a deep desire to find the man or woman of your dreams to add extra meaning to your life. Your empty days and nights can be a thing of the past. Cast away your sadness and join with so many other satisfied people who have found fulfillment through *Happy Hearts*— call in today and find an understanding and compassionate human on the other end of the line. They will help you connect with the perfect companion for you."

2. **Forceful:** Other times, the announcer needs to be forceful:

"Folks! Listen Up! This is news you have to hear! For one day, and one day only, *Roadland* car dealership is having our annual blowout sale. You *can't* beat the deals. You won't find prices this low anywhere else on the planet! You will drive away shaking your heads in wonder at the amount of money you saved. And bring a trade-in. Drive it in! Tow it in! Get your friends to push it in! If it has wheels, we'll take it! But remember, one day only! Don't delay!"

3. **Mellow:** Or you may be interviewing for the 1 a.m. to 6 a.m. show. You will be playing nothing but the mellowest of music:

"Hello, you sleepless wonders. Too much on the go? Can't get those lids to stay closed? I'm the Mellow-maker, here to bring you the softest sounds from the quiet music vault. We'll travel together through the gentle vocals of Rosemary Clooney, Harry Nilssen, Otis Reading, Al Green, Whitney Houston, Sarah McLachlan, and more. Put your cares by your bedside, turn down the lights, and sink into a soft pillow. Wind down with me until you dream the dreams of the calm and peaceful. Let's begin with this old favorite of mine. . . ."

4. **Upbeat:** Or you may be auditioning for the all-purpose announcer who takes the morning commuters through the news, sports, weather, and local interviews in an upbeat voice:

"Hey there, morning friends. Welcome back to another day in life. Another Monday morning have you down? Is traffic crawling along? Got a big report to tackle first thing? Let me pick you up. No worries at all. We have all the uplifting news you need from a rosy weather report and big wins in local sports, to an unexpected major grant to our fair city, and an interview with a comedian that you simply won't want to miss. So toss out those blues, my friends, and let me be your next cup of perky coffee."

Competence and Confidence

What we know about influence is that perception is one of the keys to success in negotiations. When you look nervous and unsure, your fellow negotiators simply will not buy that you are the person or company they can rely on to fill their needs. Or, they take advantage of your perceived weakness and play win-lose negotiating. Either way, not good! If you look confident (even if you are not feeling that way), people perceive you as competent. It just works that way.

So, while we heartily encourage you to constantly increase your knowledge and skills in your area of expertise and in the art and skills of negotiating, practicing the visual presentation skills in this section will have others more receptive to your message.

Composed Beginning

From the moment that eyes and ears are observing you, judgments and opinions are being formed. Humans form visual opinions in the first three to five seconds. And it takes just 12 to 15 seconds to also be judged vocally.

Unfortunately, the old adage is true: "You don't get a second chance to make a first impression."

So, no matter whether you are entering a room to start a session or starting within the room from a seated position, you need to look composed. You need to be "The Expert."

Strong Stride

Whenever walking, walk tall with a good straight posture. Walk in your natural gait or practice a more professional stride if you currently slouch. Watch where you are walking to avoid a mishap. Even a slight stumble gives a message of lack of control. You should scope out the room beforehand, if possible, to look for the most direct route to wherever you are going in the room. If you shake hands, make it firm enough, based on the other negotiator's behavior style: strong for a Doer, enthusiastic for a Talker, middle firm for Thinkers, and equal to theirs for Guardians.

Leader's Stance

When you arrive to wherever you will greet the person in any room, set the standard for stability and purposefulness by assuming the power position or leader's stance. This is really quite simple but powerfully effective. Stand with good, straight posture. Women, place your feet hip-width apart. It is also acceptable to have one foot slightly in front of the other. Men, place your feet shoulder-width apart. Remember to stand tall as you greet the other(s).

Tip: If you tend to have nervous feet (feet that tend to wander on their own), spread your feet just a few inches farther apart.

You are now in a steady and stable position via your feet and legs. One additional point: place your arms calmly by your side after shaking with the other. There are two reasons why doing this is effective.

First, it keeps your hands apart. Many people's nervousness shows as they do innumerable distracting things with their hands and fingers (twirling their rings, hands in pockets, hands clasped militarily behind their backs, cracking knuckles, men fig leafing, etc.).

Second, when you gesture (coming in a little while), your gestures are bigger and more communicative coming all the way up from your side rather than when your hands are clasped in front of you. If you are seated, the resting place for your hands is on the table in front of you. You will continue to gesture but will put your hands down in between to break up the energy.

Breathe

Why? When you rush into talking, people can perceive that as nervousness. And often it is. If you are not a confident and seasoned negotiator, that will likely be seen as a weakness. If you want to purposefully rush in to create excitement, that is something different. So breathe. Taking two long deep breaths helps in a number of ways. You oxygenate your cells and that has a calming effect. You can take the time to do what we call *owning the room*. It is your party and you start it when you are good and ready (not when your nervousness dictates).

Eye Connection

While you are powerfully standing in your leader's stance and taking a few wonderfully slow, deep breaths, your connection deepens with the other negotiator(s). You give them eye contact. People are aware of being connected with through eye contact. They can also feel left out, even if subconsciously, if you do not connect with them in this way. They can also perceive you as avoiding or uncomfortable. Weakness in any form.

How you make eye contact and how long you hold it depends on your circumstances. If you are one on one, you will connect more frequently. If you are in front of more people, you will look at negotiators in various seats, distributing your eye connection around the space. You are there to influence people. So "be" with them. Remember the presenter's axiom, "100 percent inclusion." Do not leave anyone out. If there is a primary negotiator or decision maker, give him or her more eye contact than the others. If it is a group negotiation, the others are not being paid to be there for their good looks. They will be decision influencers at some point during or right after the sessions. Distribute your amount of eye contact situationally.

Expressive Face

Dr. Mehrabian tells us that when face-to-face, about 60 percent of the believability is based on what we are seeing. And when we are talking with other humans, most of us look people in the eyes. As we look into eyes, we are also taking in the face. And what the face is doing or not doing gives us clues to the meaning behind the words and vocals. Everything is interconnected. So paying more attention to your face has practical applications for practical outcomes.

Monoface is just as boring as monotone. Studies at the Harvard School of Medicine found that with our hundreds of muscles, we can make approximately 7,000 different faces. So consciously use your face to your greatest positive influential advantage. Practice, as always, is needed.

Let me give you an example. With growing up in severe surroundings in New York, for self-protection I developed a stern-looking monoface. You were not easily going to read what I was thinking (that could have brought on even more trouble). I was even called *Stoneface* by one of my less kind teachers. That face became a way of life for 40 years. Then I met my warm and sweet wife. Guess what? That practiced puss was not gonna fly with this loving woman. Well, I know that with practice, I can improve anything. So I began practicing a smile. Took small steps at first. My muscles were long used to one way of behaving and my brain was programmed to have them do exactly that. So I had to retrain my brain (create new wiring connections) and exercise facial muscles that had not been called on for four decades. My face literally hurt for a few months with the new usage. But employing more of the 7,000 faces possible has achieved two basic things: I can now make *lots* of faces (at will) and I am also much more aware of what my face is doing and therefore what it might possibly be conveying—all quite useful when bargaining with people who are subconsciously relying on reading my face for clues as to how things are going.

This is not a small ingredient in face-to-face sessions. I invite you to begin a practice of paying attention to what your face is doing at least five times a day for at least two weeks until the practice begins to become a conscious habit.

Body Language and Gestures

Keeping Dr. Mehrabian's studies in mind, approximately 60 percent of your believability comes through how people perceive you visually. You can wow them or disconnect with them. Let me show you how to avoid disconnecting and enhance your verbal and vocal message.

First, the power position or leader's stance is a huge ally for you as is the seated power position. You look poised and competent. You are standing or sitting still (movement will come later) and not fidgeting. Hands are controlled and you are ready to communicate. You will use your head, body, arms, and legs to do this.

Most negotiators spend all their time preparing just the nuts and bolts and never give any thought to how they look and what their body movements communicate. But communication is at the heart of negotiations, so you better use all aspects intelligently.

The most readily available physical features for most of us are our arms, hands, and heads. So we concentrate on gestures here. Gestures have meaning. They are purposeful. They are in sync with and support our words. Here are five guidelines:

1. Your sitting gesture box will be from the table up to just under your chin and out as far as your arms can go on either side without hitting anyone.

2. You can use gestures to indicate direction, size, and sequence of events as you speak.

3. Hold your gesture for long enough that people can see it as you add to what you are saying. Stop the gesture and gently drop your hands back to the table for a moment when that gesture no longer applies until your next gesture.

4. Use your whole hand versus a pointing finger. A full hand with palm open has a greater visibility and strength and is seen as friendlier than a single finger.

5. When you motion toward or indicate a fellow negotiator, also use your full hand. Many people were raised to regard being pointed at as accusatory or rude.

Presenting Your Case Summary

Although most negotiators focus only on the products, services, and money to be traded, you can now see that how you present your arguments has a great deal to do with how the flow of communication will go. The three major components of effectiveness, the visual, vocal, and verbal elements, are consequential. Every tool that you can bring to bear for getting what you want and need in win-win negotiating will move you closer to achieving your goals. You know to take your behavior style and the style of the other(s) into consideration. You have the 4 A's Setting Direction structure to get off in a productive way. You have the tools to practice your vocals over the next days, weeks, months, and years to be ever more interesting and persuasive. And constantly practicing more powerful ways to sit and gesture will add greatly to your effectiveness as a communicator in your sessions.

Questions to Ponder
- What are your current strengths via behavior styles in presenting your case?
- What differences do you need to overcome when presenting your arguments to negotiators with differing or even opposite behaviors?
- What will it be like for you to purposefully invite out the other parties' pain points?
- How will you practice asking negative-based, powerful, open-ended questions?

- What will you need to do to become more comfortable in taking charge by setting the direction of the session from the very start?
- What will you do (and when) to change your pitch or inflection to be viewed as more interesting?
- When will you practice changing up the pace of your speech to get better at diminishing negatives and emphasizing positives?
- What will it take for you to insert more pauses before and after important bits of information, even in everyday conversations?
- What will it sound like to strengthen the projection of your voice to ensure a perception of certainty and expertise?
- How will you amp up your interest level or passion for the products and services you are in a negotiation to exchange?
- How will you become more conscious of what your body is communicating to others?
- What will it take for you to practice purposeful gesturing to increase the chance that people will more fully understand what you are saying?

Goals for Success

From the answers you get to the questions above, write S.M.A.R.T. goals that will lead to greater success in presenting your case.

S.M.A.R.T. Goals for Presentation Success

S. pecific

M. easurable

A. ctionable

R. elevant

T. ime Bound

I will _____

The Negotiating Process

8

Understanding Negotiation Fundamentals

Negotiation Fundamentals

Just as there are human fundamentals intricately involved in each and every negotiation between people, there are also negotiation fundamentals. No matter what industry, business, or department you are in, no matter the product or service being traded, these negotiation fundamentals are likely to be present. Let's begin the next level of study together.

Assumptions

An assumption is a belief or guess that something is what you think it is. But there is an absence of actually knowing. Think about that. How often have you "thought" you knew something that you came to realize was incorrect—not knowing? What are the consequences of acting on a belief or an assumption that is inaccurate or simply not true? Assumptions are all around us and have been for as long as mankind has been communicating with others (and communication is at the heart of negotiating).

For example, a commonly held assumption that you know about is that people used to think or assume that the world was flat. The old joke goes like this: "Can you name the four ships that sailed with Columbus?" Many of us had three ships drilled into us in school: The *Niña*, the *Pinta*, and the *Santa Maria*. And after proudly spouting those names, people scratch their head in wonder and say, "I thought there were only three ships." And you reply with the punch line, "The fourth ship went over the edge." Even when a whole population believes (assumes) something is so, that does not make it true.

The problem is not so much that we have mental assumptions (remember Chapter 2 and our neuron/dendrite programming and how that guides our thoughts—in this case, almost everyone had neurons that held the information given to them that the world was flat). It is when we act on an incorrect assumption that problems arise. What problem might "the world is flat" hold for populations of humans? Trade makes the world go round. We were interdependent, even back in olden days. Sailing ships went from port to port bringing goods to sell and buying new goods to fill their holds to sell at the next port. Given that the earth was flat as a matter of assumed course, Europeans knew that to get Chinese silk, they had to travel thousands of overland miles to procure it. So in this case, what they did not do was to explore the oceans to find shorter ways to get what they wanted. They were too afraid of the sea monsters waiting at "the edge" (another belief/assumption).

Let's go for a smaller assumption example than a big mass-held one like a flat earth. We sometimes hold assumptions based on stereotyping, a form of assumption. I was walking along an isolated stretch of road near the Golden Gate Bridge a few years ago when I saw a group of five young men, perhaps 18 or 19 years old, approaching from the opposite direction. I noticed that I immediately went into fear and caution mode. They were, you see, Latino. My fight-or-flight system was activated. I "assumed" the worst of these men, whom I had never even laid eyes on before. Using my New York upbringing, I walked as far right on the road as I could and averted my eyes. So I was somewhat startled to hear a friendly "Hello" and looked up to see one of the men genuinely smiling in my direction. In that moment, my assumption was busted. My mind had made up a story that all young Latino men were dangerous. And then I believed my own story. I turned the false "fact" into an assumption. I almost missed an opportunity to connect with some nice guys.

Perhaps an even more common example is something like the following. You have asked your wife/husband/friend to go to a particular restaurant a couple of times and each time they've said no and perhaps given their reason. Even though it is your favorite place, you have given up asking because you "know" what their answer will be. So you do not get what you want (at least with them). But the problem is that we assume that their past answer is and will always be their only answer. But people change. People grow. People can have new preferences and choices.

There is a certain wisdom in "not beating a dead horse." But when larger issues are at stake (in negotiations), assuming that what was true in the past is still true today will wreak havoc on finding new possibilities.

In life and in negotiations, the two secrets about assumptions is to first notice that you have one. Know that you really do not know. The second is to check out your assumption. Either validate that it is true or discover that it is not true. Asking questions is the handiest form of research (and we cover how to ask powerful questions in Chapter 12). The other party knows what is true for them.

For instance, in past negotiations with a particular vendor, you have always felt hurried in the process. Your likely assumption, then, based on past experience, is that this upcoming negotiation will also be hasty. That is a pressure that does not serve you or the process. But this time, you notice your assumption and decide that the stakes are too high to operate from guessing that what happened in the past will happen again this time. When you explore the topic with them in your early Discovery Phase (Chapter 12), you learn that the reason for the other party's past rushed behavior was that their boss was a deadline tyrant and put that pressure on your negotiating partner. But that boss is now gone and the new one knows the value of taking a bit more time to be more thorough in bargaining. Now you are updated; your old assumption can be tossed away. New possibilities arise.

The bottom line about assumptions is to stop guessing (assuming) and explore the belief/assumption. With a change in your awareness and practice, the updated yield over time will be sizable.

Information Is Power

Negotiations are usually a series of actions that involve information. The more information you bring to your awareness about goals, pressures, time lines, and tradable concessions (your own and those of the company), the clearer the negotiation process will be.

Likewise, the more information you uncover about the other party, the better prepared you are to negotiate intelligently for what you want, and for what they want. Remember, your negotiations are based on getting mutually beneficial outcomes.

The Preparation Phase (Chapter 11) gives you lots of directions for doing a better job of gathering internal information (yours and your organization's) and doing more due diligence about the other negotiating party and their organization. Likewise, industry trends, scarcity or abundance of supporting resources, internal and external political climates, national or global influences, and so on, will all be factors worth investigating.

But remember that information by itself is basically worthless. For example, if you are like most of us, you read thousands and thousands of pages of textbook material in your academic life. How much of that information have you retained? And how much of that do you use in practical ways? We are in a vast and endless communication age. And that is not going away. Thankfully, we can now access information before, during, and after negotiations in ways never before dreamed of.

When it comes to information-gathering, time management is always an issue. You have *lots* to do at work in addition to any particular negotiation. One of the biggest problems expressed to me globally when delivering the Negotiating Success training program is that "I don't have time to do enough preparation." I know the feeling. Still, you have got to do what you can. Wisdom in prioritizing your allotted time is critical. Focus first on the information boulders. If you have more time, look at the information rocks. And if you have all the time in the world, dig deeper to find the information pebbles and sand.

You will have to pick and choose among all your other duties how much time you can and will spend in hunting down "useful" information. Lack of relevant information will surely come back to bite you.

So, information is power . . . if used intelligently. Let us move on to how information is (or is not) traded in negotiations.

Disclosure Establishes Trust

Have you ever been in a conversation, relationship, or negotiation where the other person does not share much information? What is it like trying to proceed in any effective fashion? No information exchange, no movement!

And what about the times you have been with someone and they are a completely open book, telling you way more than you really need to know? Does that give you an advantage and the other a disadvantage? (By the way—advantages are absolutely fine in negotiating; you do need to get good-enough outcomes to satisfy your needs. But remember, if the others feel disadvantaged, how will that change their negotiating behavior? Will they rise up to compete in win-lose mode? Will they stay quiet this time, take a loss but come back like a lion next time? Balance and mutuality remain the keys.)

Negotiations are a dance. And there are no perfect steps. But one step that is essential is disclosure of information. The question is always when and how much to reveal. Great negotiators hold mutuality at the heart of the dance. More often than not, the more you reveal, the more the other party will trust you and so reveal back to you. Reciprocity! But you must stay tuned to what is coming back to you. A somewhat even exchange is critical so that you do not give it all away. Unfortunately, many people have been raised on win-lose and will simply try to take advantage of you.

Different behavior styles will also need to be dealt with situationally when it comes to disclosure. All of us have been trained to various degrees on how much or how little to reveal in life. Lots of us got punished as kids for too much information getting to our parents or teachers. That tends to make one cautious in disclosing information.

Trust is at stake. There is more information to help you with this in Chapter 4. Part of what puts people in this or that behavior style is based on their degree of openness. So stay tuned for more to come.

Overly Competitive = Lose-Lose

No sane person would want to come out of a negotiation with a lose-lose outcome. Yet, unknowingly, it is done all the time. Human beings are not nearly as conscious as we would like to believe. We are raised on lose-lose almost from birth. But many will call it win-lose.

Two common and strongly reinforced examples of win-lose are sports competitions and politics. In many if not most sports, an individual or team either wins or it loses. And even if there is a second or third place, if the first place "winner" is present, does second or third place really seem like winning? Political races also involve one winner and a number of "losers." In many societies, this win-lose is the norm and so ingrained that it just seems like that is how it is. The problem in negotiations is that this win-lose training simply does not work well.

So the concept of win-lose is fairly clear even if not effective. Lose-lose is when neither negotiating party gets what they want. In the end, it is really no different from win-lose and here is why. A large portion of negotiations are done with the same person and the same company over time, repeatedly. If you "lose" in a negotiation while another person "wins," do you think that will inspire you to be more collaborative, more mutuality minded next time? No! You will most likely get even more competitive. You will reveal less information, work less cooperatively, look out for good old number one because that is what the other party has done before and you assume they will do again. So you will come out with another win-lose. And so the downward spiral continues.

Collaboration, not competition, is the key to negotiating success!

Trading Value—Concessions

Concessions in a negotiation are all the things that are tradable. Money, products, and services are the big three, though they are composed of almost unlimited variety. Negotiations are a dance, a step-by-step exchange of information and tangibles. So you need to be very intelligent about what you are trading and what it is worth to you and to the other.

The ideal is to *trade what is of low cost to you and of high value to the other*, and vice versa.

For example, let us say that you are selling your home. The potential buyer asks if the washer and dryer are going with you or staying. You have already determined that it is time for a new washer and dryer when you get to your new home. So you ask a few questions to see what value the buyer may be placing on the machines. If they are hoping that you will leave them, you can come back to the machines later in the trading process and throw them in, in exchange for something that you want. (Do not assume—they may in fact be hoping that you will take them because they recently purchased a new pair and do not want to deal with the time and expense of removing yours.) But if each of you comes out with what you want, magic!

It is up to you to determine every possible product, service, or monetary feature that you have to trade. We help you with this in Chapter 11. What does your organization have to offer that you have already spent the time and money on to have in place for your operations? We call them *skill-sets*, *resources*, and *developed systems*. Most humans get into ruts. Therefore, most negotiators get into ruts. What we negotiate all the time becomes our mainly used neurons and dendrites. They are the standard "I know what I know" defaults—part of our unconscious knowing. But it is guaranteed for almost all of us that there are tradables available within our organization that we are either totally or partially unfamiliar with. Every skill-set, resource, or developed system that you fail to know about for potential trading is one less card in your hand. It is well worth the effort to do some ongoing exploration to see what is available additional to what you know now. If you felt in the past that you were fully up to speed on all the wonderful tools your organization had, might there be some new developments that in your busy schedules you simply didn't know about? Find out what they are.

And to use the skill-sets, resources, and developed systems that you already have to best advantage, you need to discover which of these items are needed by the other negotiating party. Here is a simple example but one that you can probably relate to. I was sitting at the dinner table with my son and his girlfriend. Our company needed a project completed and I was on the lookout for a resource with the right skill-set. My son's girlfriend said that she was thinking about attending bartending school. That struck a chord. A resource of mine owned a bartending school not too far away. I needed a project person and she had the skills. She needed an inexpensive bartending school and I had a connection. The bartending school connection needed coaching and I had the skills. We ended up doing a three-way swap of concessions with a win-win-win. Beautiful!

But that example is a bit haphazard. I just happened to hear about a need. In negotiations it is your job both beforehand and during the Discovery Phase to proactively uncover the other party's needs. When you have a complete list of *your* organization's skill-sets, resources, and developed systems, and you uncover the list of skill-sets, resources, and systems that the *other* party needs, you are ready to start offering and asking.

But before you go offering any of your valuables, you need to be able to put a dollar amount on their worth. Trading apples to apples (within a spectrum that you determine is good enough) is what makes for mutually agreeable outcomes. Let us use the three-way negotiation from above. The bartending school tuition was $495, and my son's girlfriend did not have that kind of money. But she did have skills we needed. I offered the owner one full hour of telephone executive coaching, even though I charge a bit less than $495 per hour. He valued that hour and could easily fit another person into a class with really no additional cost to himself. He already had the school, the instructor, and the material in place. Easy trade there. The project that my son's girlfriend did for us did not come close to being worth $495, but it was a project that needed doing. This was a favor I could do within the family, if you will. And I absolutely love using my seasoned coaching skills.

So finding what is of low cost to you but of high value to the other (and vice versa) is magic in the trading game.

Creative Thinking

In a long-term survey conducted by my company Bold New Directions, about 80 percent of people reported that they do not perceive themselves as being creative. But once we asked a few coaching questions of the hundreds involved, most people did in fact see that they have plenty of creativity. This is a blind spot well worth exposing for success in negotiations.

I have said repeatedly that negotiations are a dance, an exchange of steps between two or more parties. The key is to creatively plan your dance moves in advance and also dance in the moment as negotiations unfold. The basics steps do not change, but the music and rhythm may vary because each and every negotiation is unique. What a wonderful opportunity to take each situation and make the most of it for each side. And to do that, you need to meet each unique set of circumstances with a unique approach. And that takes creativity. While we encourage using the entire set of steps in negotiating, we strongly invite you to think, feel, and act outside the box within each of those standard steps.

Exercise: But how do you get ever more creative? Let us start with an activity that we use in our training programs (including Negotiating Success). From wherever you are, pick a city that is some thousands of miles of miles away. Imagine that you need to get there—physically get there (no "Beam me up Scotty"). How would you travel to that city? Most people first answer "Plane." Suppose there is a pilot's strike. How else could you physically get there? (Make a mental or written list.) Most people think of around 15 ways. How did you do?

But there are ways to help your brain uncover more possibilities. The brain stores information in pockets of neurons. And dendrites allow neurons to talk with each other. So *brainstorming, mind mapping,* or whatever you like to call it, invites one thought to connect with another. More possibilities emerge to consider using (later on). If you are not regularly practiced in brainstorming, notice that your analytical mind may start to play the "that won't work" game. That is a practical and necessary skill but do not allow the mind to rule out possibilities during the brainstorming process. The brainstorming's flow stops if you switch focus to viable practicalities instead of building a list of possibilities. Come back and analyze *after* the brainstorming.

Let us get back to the exercise. (Have some fun with this. Get wild and crazy.) Look at your initial list of ways to get to the city you choose. Because "flying" is usually on there. We start with that. Flying means humans in the air. Allow your brain to search around for any words (from your left brain) or images (from your right brain) of human beings in the air (remember, forget practicality for now). If you think you have exhausted the list, ask your brain for at least two more. Part of creativity is noticing when part of you wants to stop. The key is to keep going past what you think are your limits. More options usually present themselves.

How many more possibilities did you come up with?

But wait, there is more! On your original list there are usually some items that have wheels (car, bus, train, etc.). Ask your brain to muse on any kind of contraption that has wheels and can carry a human being (again, keep a mental list or, even better, write/type these down).

What did you add to your growing list?

Let us keep going. Many people will have answered "walk" when first asked how to get to that distant city. Let your mind consider anything with legs, human or otherwise (like riding a horse, etc.). Go for more now.

What did you add?

Last for this particular creativity exercise . . . what about travel associated with water? "Ship" often comes up in the first round. Picture human beings moving with water involved. Let your brain send you words and images associated with oceans, lakes, and rivers.

How did you do?

If you skimmed over this exercise . . . well, the old "nothing ventured nothing gained"; creativity insights in this case. When you get an "ah ha" about the process of creativity, you are more likely to make being more creative a regular, even daily practice in life (we come back to how this helps in negotiations in a moment).

Here are some answers that have been shouted out in our classes around the globe:

Air: Jets, propeller plane, helicopter, hang glider, parasailing, parachuting, shot from a cannon, blimp, dirigible, space shuttle, jet packs, helium balloons tied to a chair (remember the southern Californian who actually tried that one), hot air balloon, tied to a flock of birds (obviously ruled out later, but hey, his brain was cooking creatively—that is when some new ideas are born), and from a class in Saudi Arabia, "magic carpet."

Wheels: Car, bus, train, truck, RV, ATV, wagon (red and Conestoga), golf cart, wheelchair, chariot (now we are thinking out of the box), rickshaw, riding lawnmower, shopping cart, to name a few.

Legs: Walk, run, hop, skip, jog, jump rope, piggyback, horse, cow, mule, donkey, elephant, camel (two types), dog sled (a combination), giraffe, oxen, bull, zebra, ostrich (interesting that this one always seems to come up), and more.

Water: Boat, canoe, row boat, speed boat, ship, catamaran, sailboat, submarine, water ski, swim, kayak, raft.

How did your list compare? If you had some really different ones, good for you!

You see, if I had given you all these answers up front, you would probably have simply read them. Reading someone else's information may have usefulness but does nothing to encourage your own creative process. In fact, it stifles it (unless you use the information to springboard into a creativity session).

So why spend so much time on creativity in a book on negotiations? Doing the practical in negotiations is essential. Preparation, steps, phases . . . all necessary. But what happens when negotiators get "positional"? Positionality is when one or both parties get stuck in needing to have things done in a particular way. There is a difference between declaring that there is only one way to get there with being clear about what "there" is. When parties get positional or stuck, either conflict or stagnation ensues.

We call the creativity exercise presented to you the *18 Ways* process. We have classes say out loud and in unison, "There are 18 ways to do anything," to lock in the attitude and practice. There are not always 18 ways to proceed, or 18 options; sometimes there are less and sometimes there are more. But if you cultivate the attitude and practice to regularly look outside the box that your programed neurons and dendrites are automatically creating, you are much more likely to find solutions when just a little while before, there appeared to be none.

Just like having more company skill-sets, resources, and developed systems at your fingertips to consider offering, it also helps to have a creative thought process that can connect those concessions to your current negotiation scenario.

A very useful phrasing that can move negotiations along or get things started again is "What if. . . ." You are tossing in possibilities, options for consideration. And even if that item is not what the other wants, the offering can start a conversation for a series of suggestions to be considered.

Another way to get concessions considered is to say, "If we can do this (_____) for you, will you do that (_____) in return?" You are now working with the Principle of Reciprocity.

It is when you seem to run dry with things to trade that you can kick into creative mode. Note that it can help to take a break and then come back with some fresh ideas.

Think about the three-way win-win-win situation described earlier in which my son's girlfriend wanted to go to bartending school. If I sat at the table in a traditional mind-set, I might have said, "If you want to go to bartending school, you need to work hard and save up your money." Although that is one way to go about getting her needs met, there are at least 18 other ways to achieve her goal, too. And we creatively came up with an answer that worked best for all three parties. A trifecta! Nice!

Here are the last suggestions on increasing your skill at creativity. If you do the same things over and over again, that is how you have programmed your brain. Neurons that are wired together fire together. Same thoughts, same motivating feelings, with the same old results. Reduced success if you will. If you want to proactively lead creativity in negotiation sessions, it is best to practice creativity all the time.

Here are some ways to start being an ever-more-creative person and professional. Make it a practice to do *five things differently* every day. And it is easy to do. Start your day with this declaration, "Today I will find ways to do things differently at least five times." If you always set your alarm for the exact same time, change that by 5 or 10 minutes. If you put your left leg into your pants first, insert your right leg first instead. Tie your right shoelace first? Left first next time. Button your shirt top to bottom? Button it from bottom to top. Pick up your coffee with your right hand? Try your left for a change (do not burn yourself). Drive the same route to work every day? Take a different way. (And enjoy the new scenery. And, yes, do manage your time.) The possibilities are almost endless. Every time you shake things up, you are in new awareness. You force your brain to work in new ways using new neuronal pathways and firing.

Have fun with expanding how you do things. Uncomfortable at first? Just notice that and be willing to be a little uncomfortable in service to your greater good. No one yet has died of this kind of discomfort. The more you practice creativity on a regular basis (five times a day for days, weeks, months . . . life), you will absolutely notice that when you need it most (like in negotiations), you will have more easily accessed creativity at your command. It is enjoyable and effective. What a motivating combination.

Understanding Negotiation Fundamentals Summary

What are likely to show up in every significant negotiation are assumptions, degrees of use of information, trust issues, competitiveness, trading concessions, and varied use of creativity.

As we finish with negotiation fundamentals, it is a good time for you to self-assess your current strengths and weaknesses with these negotiation basics. Every single one of us can improve from wherever we are on any given skill area or character trait. For life! The Questions to Ponder section invites you to get consciously clear on where you currently excel and where the areas of opportunity are for your improvement.

Questions to Ponder
- What assumptions can I catch myself making every day?
- How has acting from assumptions failed me?
- What assumptions do I need to stop making in upcoming negotiations?
- Where do I get my information?
- Do I give myself enough time to prepare and gather information?
- How will outcomes change if I use my information more wisely?
- What are my current patterns around sharing information?
- If I hold back information, does that add to or decrease trust?
- How does sharing more openly affect the trust factor?
- How does my competitiveness affect the other party's behavior?
- What will the other party do next time if they felt they lost this time?

- Do I trade what is low cost to me but of high value to the other?
- What skill-sets, resources, and developed systems can I offer?
- How do I currently view my creativity quotient?
- What will I do on a daily basis to grow my creativity?
- How will I be more creative in future mutuality-based negotiations?

Goals for Success

From the answers you get to the questions above, write S.M.A.R.T. goals that will lead to greater success with negotiation fundamentals.

S.M.A.R.T. Goals Regarding Negotiation Fundamentals

S. pecific

M. easurable

A. ctionable

R. elevant

T. ime Bound

I will _____

9

Creating Range and Alternatives

We spent the first section of this book digging deeper into the complex human factors involved in negotiations. Now it is time to turn our attention to the nuts and bolts of negotiating. These are the skills, steps, and phases used when negotiating with others. You can apply any or all of the ingredients based on what your negotiations call for. Simple negotiations need only this or that skill, step, or phase. Long and complex negotiations will benefit greatly from your using every tool possible. Let us get started by exploring the powerful benefits inherent in the subject of creating range and alternatives.

There are five interacting components when creating a range and series of alternatives: wish, starting point, bottom line, BATNA, and WATNA.

Why is a range necessary? In negotiations, there is give and take. So there needs to be a range to move between. This applies not only to monetary factors but to any product or service you are trading as concessions. How much of any item are you willing and able to offer?

Monetary example. You are buying a rental property. You have worked with your banker and real estate agent and are clear that the *most* you can spend is $750,000. But if you can purchase the property for $675,000, you will have $75,000 to make improvements or use otherwise.

Knowing that the selling party will want to negotiate, you certainly do not start with what you can spend—the $750,000—because that does not leave any "wiggle room." So you create a monetary range that starts lower than the $750,000 but has the higher number of $750,000, which will be the limit of how much you will go. In this case, $650,000 could be your opening offer so you can still easily pay $675,000 and still have the upgrade money.

Nonmonetary example. First, nonmonetary is a misnomer. Just about everything in a negotiation aside from goodwill has a monetary value to it. And you better know what it is. Still, let us play with a range for noncash purposes.

In the case of purchasing a rental property, you would make a list of anything and everything that you want in the house. Perhaps the current owner will repaint some or the entire interior. Will they use their connection with a local landscaper to replace some of the dying foliage as part of the agreement? Can you get them to replace the rusting fence? And on and on and on.

Let us look at how wish, starting point, bottom line, BATNA, and WATNA work interactively for your success.

Wish

People have an internal thought process. When it comes to internal negotiations, we often negotiate ourselves down. For example, "I don't think my boss will give me that much of a raise." "Ryan usually says no when I ask for that so I won't ask again." "The owner of that property will never go for that." That is a diminishing process.

The wish is designed to help us think big at first. Really big! This number or idea is generally a bit unrealistic. But here's the good news. Thinking big in the Preparation Phase helps you to begin with a higher starting point. No one but you ever knows this number or idea. It is an unspoken, internal-to-you process only, done before the actual negotiations begin.

Example—Buyer. You want to purchase that rental property and you know the asking price of $725,000 is within neighborhood norms. But if you first offered $725,000, you know the response is going to be that they ask for more. So how much lower do you go and how do you get to the best start? By thinking *big*! Imagine, just imagine, that the current owner is in dire straits and your fantasy is that if they can only get $500,000, their financial worries will dissolve. So your wish is that you can buy the property for $500,000. The more you think about that number, the more mentally/emotionally comfortable you will be with it. Just let that number sit for a while.

Example—Seller. If the sellers are skilled in negotiating, they will be going through the same process. They will also come up with a wish so that they do not start off on the wrong foot with nowhere to go to make up for a bad starting point. Expanding their vision might be like this: "My research has shown that the average local market value for properties like mine puts the price at $725,000. But what an investment! It will surely be worth *lots* more as the neighborhood is on the upswing. In my dreams [wish], I would get $1,000,000 for this fine place. I will ruminate on that number so that it feels good (even though I know it is not the number I will first suggest)."

Remember—at this earliest, prenegotiation stage, think *big*!

Starting Point

Depending on whether you are the buyer or seller, the *starting point* will be the least you can "realistically" expect to pay for something or the most you can realistically expect to receive for something. This is the top of a seller's range (or the bottom of a buyer's range). And, unlike the wish, this number is based on due diligence, real-world numbers. But you have been sitting with a *big* number in your head ($500,000 as buyer, $1,000,000 as seller) so that you do not start too low or high, therefore leaving potential money on the table. You do not want to be laughed out of the room or seem to disrespect the other party, but you create a stretch figure within the outer borders of reality (and you will need to justify that number to the other party). You (the buyer) decide that you will offer $650,000.

Who Names the Number First?

I am using the money (Number) factor as the example, but this concept can apply to all tradables.

There are two general rules of thumb about who names the first number. Unfortunately, they are opposite strategies. You will need to situationally decide which route to go.

1. "Whoever names the number first loses." This was the first rule I learned and it has validity. Using the real estate example, let us assume for a moment that this is a private sale and the price has not been listed publicly (real estate can be a bit different from many other negotiations). The typical dance is that one party says to the other, "So what price did you have in mind?" Now if they name one, they've possibly made it easier (more to come). Why? Because you now know the ballpark they want to play in. And it may be pleasantly surprising. There is no backing away from that starting point for the other. If the seller names a price first and it is $750,000, they cannot later ask for more than $750,000 (unless you have negotiated that because of lots of add-ons). They are stuck with their starting point with usually nowhere to go but down.

2. "Name the price first." Why do this? The primary reason is that it can change (and sometimes dramatically) the other party's expectations. If the property owners prepared well,

knows local listings are in the $725,000 range, and are hoping to get a bit more than that, what do you imagine will happen to their thinking if you start by offering $650,000? For all but the most hardnosed negotiators, this much lower figure will change their expectations of what they can get from you. You will more likely lower their expectations. You have changed the playing field.

There is no one perfect approach. You need to know who you are dealing with. What is your economy's precedence? What might be changing? What is at stake in your deal?

Remember, too, that this applies to all tradables, not just to the monetary factor. If you came into the session wanting to occupy the building in approximately six months after selling another property you own and the seller wants to complete the deal within 60 days, expectations change. If you thought you could get them to paint the interior but discover they are moving to Hawaii in a month with no time for that kind of commitment, expectations change. And so on. Every negotiation has different factors. Each needs to be approached situationally.

Bottom Line

This is your walkaway point. You will go no higher than (if you are buying) or lower than (if you are selling). Have you ever exceeded what you said was your bottom line? When I ask this question globally in our Negotiating Success training program, the majority of people say yes. We cover this again in a little while.

Using the real estate negotiation, you have crunched all your numbers and determined that $750,000 is all that you will commit to this project. That's it! That is your walk-away point.

So, the range you have created to work within is a starting point of $650,000 and a bottom line of $750,000. You have $100,000 of wiggle room.

BATNA—Best Alternative to a Negotiated Agreement

This fourth element in Creating Range and Alternatives is when there is no deal possible with the current other party. You have tried your best but it is not going to happen.

Again, have you ever gone past your bottom line in previous negotiations? Given more than you said you would or accepted less than you said you wanted?

That *never* needs to happen again (okay, a little dramatic, but very possible). Your BATNA will be your safety net. Here is how it works.

During the Preparation Phase, you determine your starting point and bottom line. Here is the addition. You also plan in advance for the possibility that the deal will not go through—that they will not accept even your bottom line. Well, there is no need to cave in. You have already thought of what your alternatives are if there is no negotiated agreement. You have options. These are your safety nets.

Real estate—your starting point as buyer is $650,000 and your bottom line is $750,000. You really like and want that property. But that property is not the only solution to your desire to own a rental property. It is "one" solution. You want a rental property, of a certain size, for a certain amount of money, in a certain geographical area. And you would like it around now in your life.

But the key for inner peace and outer negotiating success is to brainstorm as many (real estate) options as possible that will meet your multicriteria needs. What other buildings are on the market? (Remember: be creative. There are "18 Ways" to get what you want—including in real estate.) What other sources do you have to uncover even more options (than those listed in the multiple listings)? What other agents can you work with? Are you willing to expand your geographical preference to the next neighborhood over? Do you have the time to patiently wait for a month? Two months? The more viable options you come up with, the stronger you will feel when your bottom line is tested. If they are not the only game in town, play another game.

There are times when there is a single source supplier and your options are limited. That is the real world. As always, I say, "Use what you can, when you can, with whom you can."

WATNA—Worst Alternative to a Negotiated Agreement

As you are preparing, and after you have created as many alternative options as possible, this fifth element of Creating Range and Alternatives can be a helpful checking in anticipation of a deal possibly not going through.

The WATNA can work for you in two ways.

Using the real estate scenario, in this case, you did not get a signed agreement with the ideal property's owner. What is the worst you can imagine being the result of not getting the deal done? If you have at least one BATNA, you are relatively okay. But if in checking in with your real-life negotiation subjects, you simply cannot come up with a viable alternative for getting what you want and need, that is good to know.

If exploring your WATNA, and there are no other options, the way this helps is to go back to your bottom line and see if that truly is your bottom line. If you have no alternatives and think you may need to go past your bottom line, then it really is not your bottom line. It is now, in your Preparation Phase, best to know this and get straight about your strategy. Getting caught blindsided in the negotiation puts too much pressure on you and can have you panic into giving away more than is necessary.

Remember, all of this is first determined in the Preparation Phase, where there is much less pressure while preparing on your own. You may need to readdress this as the negotiation moves along. Conditions change and information is added as you go through almost any negotiation.

Creating Range and Alternatives Summary

When you create a wish, that makes your starting point bigger, and you can preserve your bottom line by having a clear BATNA and WATNA. You will know where you are going and be able to adjust from a place of strength.

Questions to Ponder
- Which of the five ingredients are you already strong in?
- Of the five, which have you not been using or using well?
- Which ones could you strengthen?
- What will you do to encourage yourself to think BIG for the wish?
- What habit(s) do you need to change for a strong starting point?
- Is your bottom line really your bottom line?
- How will you apply the "18 Ways" exercise to create more BATNAs?
- If using WATNA is new to you, what do you need to do to use it to reevaluate your bottom line?

Goals for Success

From the answers you get to the questions above, write S.M.A.R.T. goals that will lead to greater success in creating range and alternatives.

S.M.A.R.T. Goals for Creating Range and Alternatives
S. pecific
M. easurable
A. ctionable
R. elevant
T. ime Bound
I will _____

10

Concretizing "Why," "What," and "How"

Why, What, and How

Why are you in the negotiation? What will you trade? How will you get to where you want to be? These are the basics of every negotiation and yet many "negotiators" do not fully know the answers or do not understand the full importance of each domain. Adding clarity to these three foundational areas will bring you more success more often. They will also serve to unite the parties (build rapport) and prevent and dissolve conflict.

Why

We will start with Why you are there. This would seem so apparent but perhaps deceptively so. First, the Why of your negotiations are nonnegotiable. Simply stated, they are your needs. Second, they are composed of professional and personal ingredients as both are always at stake.

Professional: Nonnegotiable? Of course! If you are there to negotiate a new service contract with a vendor, you are not there to bargain an internal employee agreement. Duh! But it is amazing how many negotiations can get that far off track. Think of any meeting that you have been in. The meeting starts well enough, on track, on agenda. Before you know it, though, one subject leads to another and then to another and, before long, you find yourselves trying to fix every problem in the company. Our brains work via association and everything is interconnected. So it simply makes sense that we negotiators can get off track (Talkers being the most common).

How to use the Why. In your Preparation Phase, get clear about not only the main objective of your negotiation but also any subpoints that are nonnegotiable. Let us use the real estate example. What is nonnegotiable—the Why you are there. You are there to purchase a rental property. You have defined a geographical area to which you are amenable. You have a price that is defined. But let us say that during the meeting, the seller tells you about another property they have that can be bought for a song. And the photos they show you capture your imagination. And you start discussing this new property. This is how one can start getting off track. Although there are many attractive features to this new piece of real estate, it happens to be in Florida. One of your nonnegotiables is that because you will be living in one side of the duplex, it has to be in *this* town. Use your EQ and notice what you are doing in relation to what they are doing in relation to your prime negotiation goal(s).

Personal: Nonnegotiable? Yes! This is an area that most negotiators fail to appreciate. You have things about you that are nonnegotiable. One word for them is *values*. How many bargaining sessions have been thrown off track because one party trashes the values of the other?

People are not automatons. When we negotiate, we bring our whole selves to the process. But most of us have only been taught the mechanics of trading *things*. We have not learned more about the human factor as you have been doing throughout this book.

In mutuality-based negotiations, humans are at the heart of the process. Before you go into a session, remind yourself of your highest values. For example, they may be honesty, integrity, and communication. Do something different from the past. In the Discovery Phase, name these values directly to the others. Tell them you will be negotiating from these values. Ask them if they also hold these same values. If so, you have wonderful common ground established—a code of conduct. What a great way to start.

And find out what their deepest additional values are. If you know and honor each other's values, you are much more likely to respect each other. And when you respect each other, negotiations go more smoothly. If either one of you goes astray on this topic, you have permission to speak up, name it, and request a return to the initial agreement of honoring your values. That too reduces conflict.

So Why you are here is where you always return to when you are stuck in a position or go too far astray from the agreed-on agenda or set of values.

What

You are clear about the fundamental reasons for being in the negotiations. You have the business purpose mapped out and your personal needs detailed. Now you get ready for the many possible tradables exchanged.

What tangibles do you need in order to succeed from your side in the negotiations? The What is your list of tangibles. The company list will come from its products and services, skill-sets, resources, and developed systems. Your personal list will come from all the traits you have to fully offer (remember that *you* are an incredibly valuable commodity).

The other parties will also have their lists on all these counts. They may or may not be as clear as you are on yours. In win-win negotiating, you can help them clarify as you are in service throughout your time together.

Many negotiators assume that they know all that they have to offer simply because they have worked for the company. Rethink that! You have superb benefits to offer. Unless you use every single facet of the company every single day, you probably do not know or have forgotten some of the products, services, skill-sets, resources, or developed systems that are available through every department and member of the company's team. Though we come back to this in detail in the Preparation Phase (Chapter 11), let us take a peek now.

Products: Make a list of every single product your company has to offer. Write this down, even though you think you know. If you come up with even one more, you can add more value to upcoming negotiations on a situational basis.

Collaborate in this list-making. It is probable that you simply cannot know everything the company offers. Most of us unintentionally get into habits from what we do or use most often. Open up to your blind spots even as your ego may say your list is already perfect.

The short-term investment in building this list (and asking others to help keep it up-to-date) will serve immeasurably.

Skills: Mentally and physically go through every department. Tally the individual skills of the staff working there. Also look for departmental skills. This will have your brain thinking outside the box.

Services, External: Every service that supports your product or others' products.

Services, Internal: Your company has an abundance of systems and processes that support the success of your company and your customers. They are often behind the scenes and could be one of your blind spots as you may take them for granted.

Note: Go through every single item on your list. Look them over from every angle to see what makes them unique in any way.

Highlight the uniqueness and value as you look to trade them in all possible negotiations. Monetize the value. Share this list with everyone in your organization who could also use these resources to good advantage.

How

Think of a negotiation process as a journey. You are taking a trip with your family (the company). On this particular trip (or negotiation), you have a destination (your Why). Imagine you are going from Portland, Maine, to Portland, Oregon.

What will you bring along the way to ensure reaching your goal? You and your family have money, suitcases filled with items, lots of enthusiasm, and ingenuity. (In the case of your negotiation, it is your company's products, skills, and services that you have in hand.)

How will you get to Portland, Oregon? (What are the methodologies in the negotiations?) Do have a plan! You know why you are going. You know what you are bringing along to give as you go. You also need to know how you want to proceed. And, your plan must be *flexible*.

The first How is about mutuality. You are going to be collaborative.

The second How is as a leader. You will inspire accepting and honoring values, needs, differences, and mutuality. The third How is your strategy for moving things along. Think again of your trip. How will you get to Portland, Oregon? "By plane of course." Great strategy! Until there is an airline pilots' strike.

But you have a backup plan. You know that any How strategy might not pan out. So you think, "Okay, we'll take the train." Then you learn that the government just defunded Amtrak. So you ask your family (or team) to brainstorm ideas. Everyone enjoys this. You hear, "Car, bus, bike, walk, run, hitch-hike, hot air balloon, pogo stick, rickshaw, lawnmower. . . ." You are amazed at how many ways there are to get there when you get unstuck from your original plan. The same process will yield you options in a stuck negotiation or one that needs redirection.

A *flexible* plan is the key. On your family trip, if you stewed about the pilots' strike, you would still be at the airport getting nowhere. With flexibility you are never stuck. You are never positional (which is the fuel for conflict)! You do not care so deeply about one particular method, one particular pathway. You return to Why you are in the negotiation and you find other, mutuality-based ways of getting to your Why.

Concretizing Why, What, and How Summary

Your Why, What, and How are the interrelated dynamic trio of negotiations. They are the framework in which the entire negotiation process takes place. Each of the three has strength or has weakness. Pay attention to all.

Questions to Ponder
- What can you do to strengthen being the one to return the session to the mutual Whys when things go astray?
- What homework will you do to ensure a truly complete list of products, services, skills . . . the What to offer when the timing is right?
- What can you practice every day that will have you more adept at choosing and switching How you join in the negotiation process?

Goals for Success

From the answers you get to the questions above, write S.M.A.R.T. goals that will lead to greater Why, What, and How success.

(continued)

S.M.A.R.T. Goals for Why, What, and How
S. pecific
M. easurable
A. ctionable
R. elevant
T. ime Bound
I will _____

11

Preparing for Your Session

Earlier in this book, we pointed ahead to some of the five phases of negotiations. Now we are ready to unpack them fully. As you can see in Figure 11.1, there are five distinct phases: Prepare, Discover, Check In, Trade, and Evaluate. We discuss each one in turn and show how they relate to your overall negotiation.

In my broad experience, the average negotiator uses only two of the five phases in negotiations: prepare and trade. When you have learned to use all five phases and to use them well, you will be anything but average.

This is your time to get organized. You will usually be less pressured now than during the negotiation process itself. The better prepared you are going into the session, the better the outcome, plain and simple! Here are some considerations as you prepare. Make sure that you consider all of your business and personal needs.

Internal and External Preparation (Yours and Theirs)

Most negotiators prepare from only their side. Including preparation with the other negotiators in mind will reduce surprises and bring you both greater success.

FIGURE 11.1 The Five Negotiation Phases

Business—Yours *Clarify organization goals:* Remember, this is "Why" you are there. You should clearly know your major and minor goals. If you have any uncertainties, check in with the person who will be looking at your results. Go in clear!

Create and prioritize your agenda: Not everything has equal weight in a negotiation. One part influences another. What will you suggest as a starting point when the Discovery Phase begins? Do not ever assume that the other party will simply agree that this is the most important starting point. In fact, this is where *many* disagreements come from.

Range and alternatives: This is where you use all of the tools talked about in Chapter 9. Be clear; be ready!

Why, What, How: Again, if you have taken in what we covered in Chapter 10, you will be well on your way to having a great set of information and insights to bring into play during the session.

Benefit-laden resources, skill-sets, and developed systems: You and your organization have many successful business components that support your ongoing ability to sustain and grow your business. Your organization's needs are unique. There may be others similar to yours but no other entity has your exact compilation of people, resources, skill-sets, and systems. That can be a huge advantage in any particular negotiation. Trading dollars is on center stage in most negotiations. But myriad additional concessions are usually needed to complete a complex deal.

The ideal concession is one that costs little to you but is highly prized and needed by the other party. Makes sense, doesn't it? Low cost to you; high value to them. This works in reverse, too. What does the other party already have that you need? What would it cost you to start from scratch on this need?

The real estate example can be used again. Let us say you are fresh to the rental property game. In thinking through your choice to invest in a rental property, you clarify that you will need insurance people, maintenance expertise, rental agent, advertising know-how, and more. If the selling parties are wise, they will have discovered that this is your first rental property. With this information, they could try to anticipate your needs. Remember, they have already been there. They do great preparation so they are ready to offer support that they already have as part of their system. Although money may be the main object of bargaining, what can they have at the ready to sweeten the pot for leverage and satisfaction? Their list might include a specialized rental accountant, relationships with the landlord association, painters, plumbers, electricians, landscape crews, plow company, and more. When the timing is right, they can take a lot of pressure off you by offering these resources. No extra cost to them. And somehow, some way, they will want something in return. Win-win.

Another real-life example from my travels in the training world comes from work with a well-known, mega-sized global snack industry corporation. They realized that times have changed. The days of dictating to small stores about how much shelf space and location in the store were over. More competition and more enlightened customers were forcing the strategy revisit. So they started to think in terms of benefit-laden resources, skill-sets, and developed systems they already had and that smaller mom and pop grocery stores needed. These small stores simply did not have anywhere near the financial resources that this mega-corporation had. One of the items to trade, then, was massive statistics on customer buying trends. This research cost the mega-company millions of dollars to compile for its own needs. Because they already spent this money, it was low cost for them to offer the information to small grocery stores in exchange for prime shelf space/location for their own snack products. Win-win.

Expanding your knowledge of your organization's total benefit-laden resources, skill-sets, and developed systems is likely to come in handy, too. Monetizing the worth of the collected benefits will also inform you in gauging how much to offer in trade. Because you will need to spend a bit of time ensuring that your list is more complete, think of this, too, as not a one-out but to be used again and again. It will be helpful to find ways to stay up-to-date over time as your organization adds to the list.

Here are some ideas on what to look for within your organization to offer when the time is right.

Benefit-Laden Resources
- Logistics capability.
- Global coverage by market and regions.
- Scale of operations.
- Capacity utilization.
- Financial capacity.
- Better data.
- Investment in dedicated computer systems, software support, marketing, and service.

Benefit-Laden Skills
- Specialized knowledge of market segment.
- Faster response time.
- Customer relations and extra service.
- Close attention to detail.

- Professionalism.
- Experience in identifying, negotiating, and managing collaborations.

Benefit-Laden Systems
- Information systems.
- Accounting.
- Auditing.
- Forecasting.
- Quality controls.
- Customer satisfaction monitoring.
- Cash flow reporting.

This list is only a primer for you to start your own organization-centric exploration. Get the help of all who can contribute—those in the know. Your success in negotiating for your department or division ultimately serves everyone.

Business—Theirs *Clarify their organization goals:* What can you learn in advance about what the other party's goals will be? And what you cannot prepare for, you will need to find out early in the Discovery Phase.

What is their prioritized agenda? What is your best guess as to what their agenda will be (it is only a guess). This is usually revealed in the Discovery Phase. But to make the discovery process amicable, make sure to discuss each other's preferred agenda. Prioritizing agendas is first on your list of to-do's. Unfortunately, most common is for one party to launch into a line of bargaining without checking in with the second party. Not only that, but often the second party simply reacts to the first and starts bargaining about whatever the first party introduced (without agreement). What a mess. But until now, you may not have known any better. It is time to stop that madness. Discuss and agree before moving on— together. (This is often the first negotiation.)

Their range and alternatives: At least try to put yourself into their shoes. Doing so may prevent a surprise leading to a knee-jerk reaction that may not serve you.

Their benefit-laden resources, skill-sets, and developed systems: As you prepare your own organization's list of resources, skill-sets, and developed systems, look for deficits. What might the other negotiating party have that your organization could use? What might that party be putting on their list to offer you when the trading time is right? Win-win can be achieved in many ways.

Benefit-Laden Resources

- Logistics capability.
- Global coverage by market and regions.
- Scale of operations.
- Capacity utilization.
- Financial capacity.
- Better data.
- Investment in dedicated computer systems, software support, marketing, and service.

Benefit-Laden Skill-Sets

- Specialized knowledge of market segment.
- Faster response time.
- Customer relations and extra service.
- Close attention to detail.
- Professionalism.
- Experience in identifying, negotiating, and managing collaborations.

Benefit-Laden Developed Systems

- Information systems.
- Accounting.
- Auditing.

- Forecasting.
- Quality controls.
- Customer satisfaction monitoring.
- Cash flow reporting.

Personal—Yours *Negotiating style:* Take to heart the lessons of Chapter 4. You will most likely be negotiating with someone who is not your clone. Noticing your own behavioral tendencies and practicing with behavior styles all around you every day will help you in advance to read and adapt most quickly with your ever-changing negotiation partners (throughout your career).

Job motivations: No matter how good you are or how often you negotiate, each and every time you enter into a new session, your job is on the line. Before each session, take a quick review of the upcoming business to see what is at stake for you. What pressures are you feeling and from whom? If you score a big win in the negotiation, what will the outcome mean to your work life? If you come away a loser, how will that impact you? Do not take any of this for granted (and it only takes a few moments to consider).

Values: We talked about this briefly in "Why," "What," and "How." You do have values and they can be supported or crushed by your negotiating partner. When people step on each other's cherished values (again, things like honesty, integrity, openness, fairness, timeliness, respect, and a hundred others), there is conflict. If you know your own values overtly, name them at the beginning of the conversation in the Discovery Phase and ask about the other party's values. You will both have a more solid foundation to work from.

Personal—Theirs *Negotiating style:* What do you know about the other participants' style from past negotiations? What sort of information can you get from people in your network who know them? How can you take best guesses from looking at their LinkedIn profiles? Learning ever more about human behavior styles (negotiating styles) and practicing how to close the gap between you and them will serve all concerned. If the other participants are unknown to you beforehand, the faster you can read the clues and cues they are always giving off, the faster you can flex for Platinum Rule success.

Job motivations: The other party also has professional concerns or pressures. The more you learn beforehand, the better. But you can always ask them at the beginning of the conversational Discovery Phase. I ask questions like, "What would be good for me to know about your work pressures that would allow me to support you more directly in this session?" Although the other side is sometimes taken aback or hesitant as they probably have never had a question like this asked of them, when you convey how win-win related this is, most will respond with useful information. This builds trust.

Values: You do not have to guess at their values. Past experience helps, but they know the answer to this (though, again, they may have never overtly thought of or been asked about personal "values"). But when you lead the way to mutuality-based discovery and name what is important to you that you want present during your exchanges, that will spark their own needs. Agreeing about honoring values is huge glue for more peaceful sessions.

Uniting Your Team

Only you will know how often you negotiate alone or as part of a team. There are advantages and disadvantages to both.

Let us explore the five advantages of team negotiations.

1. When you gather your combined strengths, when you harness them to move in unison, you have a power that is much greater than any individual.

2. No matter how skilled and experienced you are as an individual, a team brings together a greater range of talent. Used well, this greatly expands your collective abilities.

3. There is no doubt about it, negotiations can be mentally, emotionally, and even physically tough. When you are working well as a team, you spread the challenge among you and have the opportunity to lend support to each other, particularly when the going gets rough.

4. When the other party works with you, it is less likely that proceedings will break down into personal battles when there are others on your side to buffer the situation.

5. You will often need to consult with or report to someone above you in the hierarchy. When the team has good group consensus, management is often influenced by the mass of a team's experience or collective suggestions.

The challenge of working as a team instead of as an individual is that the more people, the more complexity. Here are seven suggestions for working in more harmony for greater effectiveness.

1. As a team, review each individual's personal behavior style. Get understanding and acceptance of everyone's style. Strategize how to use the diversity to greatest positive effect.

2. Who has what authority? The time to work this out is in the Preparation Phase and not in the negotiations. Unscrupulous negotiators will take advantage of a team's lack of harmony or alignment and pit one of you against the other. Use each member's expertise to full advantage. Do not let egos undermine the collective value. A unified team with preagreements about who will address what is a powerful force. This is true especially when everyone agrees that mutuality will serve the common good.

3. Agree that one person on the team speaks at any given time. Practice Level II listening. Do not interrupt each other in front of the other party. That signals lack of teamwork.

4. As addressed earlier, conversations can easily go astray. One thing leads to another. The more people you have, the more likely this is to occur. Do not let it. Remember to appoint an internal gatekeeper to keep agreements, ground rules, and courtesies alive.

5. Help each other keep the peace. Emotions are bound to occur. Create a team code of conduct and empower everyone to remind each other when necessary.

6. Take a break when you need to. This is common sense and should be agreed on as a team before the session and also as part of the Discovery Phase with the other party.

7. Evaluate together. Each of you will remember certain parts of the negotiations in separate ways. Pool your memories and experiences *immediately* following a session. Getting everyone together again in the future is unlikely—it is best to evaluate right after the session ends.

Team negotiations can be the most powerful or the most destructive form of negotiating. You have the choice to shape the outcome.

Preparing for Your Session Summary

Preparation is the key to successful negotiations. Time is always an issue but the return on investment is well worth the extra effort. Remember to consider business and personal issues, your side and their side. Each party usually represents a much greater resource than is actually considered within more transactional negotiations. Expand your options for greater success.

Questions to Ponder
• What will inspire you to take at least a little more time to prepare?

- How will you go about gathering even more knowledge of your organization's resources for potential trade?
- What new methodologies will you use to gather greater information about the other side's organization and personal information?
- What is at stake for you professionally in your negotiations?
- What is on the line for you professionally (W.I.I.F.M. to do better)?
- What do you need to do to have more effective team negotiations?

Goals for Success

From the answers you get to the questions above, write S.M.A.R.T. goals that will lead to greater preparation success.

S.M.A.R.T. Goals for Preparation Success
S. pecific
M. easurable
A. ctionable
R. elevant
T. ime Bound
I will _____

12

Discovering All Sides

Discovery Phase

This is an absolutely critical phase. I will say that again. *The Discovery Phase is absolutely critical!*

Most negotiators do their preparation, sit competitively on the opposite side of the table (or on the other side of the phone or email), and then jump into trading (what most call negotiating). Ouch! They have missed two of three direct-interaction phases and unintentionally sabotaged their process.

This phase can make or break your negotiating success. Done well, and the rapport is built, trust established, and critical ground rules agreed on for bargaining in best fashion. Done haphazardly (or often, not at all), and you have created the proverbial "long row to hoe."

Of the three direct-interaction phases (Prepare and Evaluate are basically done before and after the "negotiation," respectively), the Discovery Phase should be the longest by far. Here is why. If you do the Discovery Phase well, the other two phases will be shorter and (much) easier. That in itself brings more success.

The biggest gift I can give you here is: *Do not allow bargaining* at this early point. *You are not ready yet!*

Let us break discovery down into its productive elements. We approach this as if you are doing it face-to-face, but the same steps apply to phone calls and even email. Again, avoid negotiations of any degree of complexity by email unless there is 100 percent absolutely no other way to do it.

You have prepared well and are now at the negotiating table (physically or by phone/video-conference). Who will start? *You* do! Lead the way immediately. Establish that you are a positive force from the very get-go. Let your face, vocals, and language convey confidence and mutuality. You set the positive tone.

From the moment you can see and hear the other parties, be taking in their physical, vocal, and verbal clues. Understand their style(s) as quickly as possible. What is their attitude? What is their mood? Where on the spectrum of human ways are you more or less in sync? Where do you sense gaps between you?

What you do or do not do now sets the stage for success or failure, conversation or conflict. Again, *do not dive into trading concessions yet*.

- You need to set and agree on ground rules.
- Do *not* assume anything.
- How long will you be together?
- Who will be the timekeeper?
- Assign a gatekeeper; or, if only two of you, agree that each of you will share this role. This person will help keep the process on track. You must empower him or her so he or she can break in; that is, comment on time, warn that you are off agenda, suggest taking a healthy break, and anything else that will facilitate success.
- Propose an agenda. Listen to the parties' thoughts and collaboratively agree to a set of prioritized areas to cover.

Warning: This is where many, many negotiations go astray and break down. One side states an initial area of concern. The other side reacts with their view or rebuts. The other side responds and deepens the discussion, which may become an argument.

Let us use the real estate example. This first pass will be how negotiation meetings often go.

Selling Party (SP): Good morning!

You: It's good to be here.

SP: What do you think of the property?

You: It's okay, but I think you are asking too much.

SP: Hey, I've put tens of thousands of dollars of improvements in over the last two years.

You: Yeah, but after the inspection, I can see that I am going to have to put in many more thousands to bring it up to my standards.

Blah, blah, blah. . . . They are off and running in all too familiar fashion. Trouble lies ahead that could absolutely be avoided. No relationship has been started or reestablished. No ground rules for how they would be with each other have been structured. No starting point (agenda) has been agreed on.

It is essential to have a framework from which the eventual bargaining nuts and bolts will be supported. When you commit to a thoughtful and complete Discovery Phase, you will spend up to 60 percent of your time here. It may seem counterintuitive at first to linger on relationship and formatting when you could simply be getting down to business. Well, creating a solid foundation *is* the business. It may just be a new way for you. That is okay. You already know that new dendrites need to be formed in your brain. You know that patience is needed to change old habits. Like anything new, work these new practices in slowly. Start with small and even personal negotiations. Perfect practice does make (more) perfect results.

Let us try this real estate meeting again, with a more robust Discovery Phase in action.

Selling Party (SP): Good morning!

You: It's good to be here.

SP: What do you think of the property?

You: I see lots of potential in it.

SP: Great! Let's talk money.

You: Well, we will of course get to talking money. But this is a major deal for both of us. Let's get some agreements in place about how we will go about discussing this so that everything is smoother.

SP (perhaps hesitantly at first): What did you have in mind?

You: Well, I find it always makes things easier if we are in sync with how we will work together. There can be disagreements that come up, but we can decide to have an adult way of being with that. It also helps if we find out each other's most important issues and then agree on what order we will talk about things. Would that be okay?

SP (perhaps still a little impatiently): Tell me more.

You: I don't know you well and I want to make sure I treat you with the kind of respect that you prefer. Tell me more about what is important to you in the relationships when you tackle real estate deals.

And on and on. . . . Start conversationally. This does not have to be a throat-grabbing win-lose interaction. Gently pull hesitant (uneducated) parties in at their highest ground level. Explain that you are starting this way because doing so will create more ease when the hard trading begins and the predictable disagreements arise. Reinforce that this will work out more positively for both of you.

As you continue your early discussion, in whatever ways you want, tell the other party "Why" you are there, business and personal. Again, this will take leadership on your part. Many negotiators never think to include the personal element even though it is always (most often silently) present. Then, find out why they are there. Do Not Assume! Do Not Let Them Assume!

The Why is critical. Once you get involved in the Trade Phase, you will often find yourself off track. When you get all the Whys out clearly in Discovery Phase, you can easily return to them (via the Gatekeeper role, please).

Discuss facts. This, too, can be a trap. We are proposing that you simply begin getting possible concessions out in the open—the wish list if you will. You will need to **break the old habit** of then starting to trade those concessions. Patience! You are still, yes still, getting the lay of the land, which means the *entire* territory. Until you know everything possible, trading now will be like "ready, fire, aim!"

So, discuss the facts . . . extensively. When you think you are done, ask an open-ended question such as, "What else would be helpful to know?" or "What is missing from our picture?" If you take productive time in the Discovery Phase, up to 60 percent of the total negotiation time, you will be able to *check in* quickly and *trade* much more clearly, swiftly, and easily.

Skills for Use in Discovery

Because you should be spending the greatest percentage of your negotiating time in this phase, it makes sense that there are a number of important skills to practice. Each of these stands on its own, but they are also interconnected over the course of communicating for information discovery.

Discovery Skill #1—Objective versus Subjective

"Objective" definition: Not influenced by personal feelings or opinions in considering and representing facts. Unbiased; impartial. Verifiable facts, if you will.

"Subjective" definition: Based on or influenced by personal feelings, tastes, or opinions.

Why is understanding the difference and differentiating these two during a negotiation important? Unfortunately, once you begin using your self-awareness and social awareness, you will discover that the greatest majority of humans pepper their interchanges with lots of subjectivity. There is nothing wrong with people adding their personal view in life. But in the business of negotiations, are you there to negotiate personal views? Your list of business Why you are there and What you will trade are typically objective. If you do not understand that most people collapse objective and subjective into an indistinguishable mélange, you will soon be off track. Although people do argue about "facts," it is opinion and judgments that cause the most disagreement. You can stop (or slow) the madness that arises in negotiations by recognizing when something said (or written) is in the land of objectivity or subjectivity.

The two keys to dealing with subjectivity, then, is to first recognize that subjectivity is on the table and then to explore it. We return to the real estate conversation in a moment. But first, let us get some common subjective examples in front of you.

Subjective terms you may hear and need to question in a negotiation:

Too Much	Immediately	Some
Not Enough	Bad	Expert
Fewer	Offensive	Excellent
More	Better	Nice
Good	Proper	High
Adequate	Quality	Low
Appropriate	Suitable	Big
Professional	Natural	Small

Subjective terms are not defined by themselves. Two parties will most often have two different interpretations about what a subjective term means. That wreaks havoc in a session and is a major source of conflict. What to do? Probe, explore, define, agree!

Let us return to the real estate discussion to pick up on some exploration of sample subjective terms.

SP: Good morning!

You: Hi.

SP: We have a *prime* property to look at today.

You: Great! Tell me more about what makes it prime for you.

SP: (Details his or her definitions.)

You: Thanks for that clarity. While I agree that it has some *great appeal*, I don't think it is *worth* what you are asking for it.

SP: Please be more specific with dollar amounts.

You: (Name a figure.)

SP: That is way *too low*.

You: What do you mean by "too low"?

SP: (Forced to name an amount.)

You: Ah, now I can see the ballpark you are in. Thank you!

SP: Do you think you will decide *soon*?

You: What time frames are you working with?

Can you see that it is probable that there are many times during a discussion when, if you are actively tuning in to subjective terms, you will find places to clarify? The good news is that once you start consciously listening for general, vague, and subjective phrasing, you will find them quite regularly. If you practice listening in everyday conversation, you will be much faster at picking up subjective terms in negotiation sessions. Asking clarifying questions will give you the information that you can work with for what we call criteria-based negotiating.

Discovery Skill #2—Empathy

Definition: The ability to understand and share the feelings of another.

What do feelings have to do with negotiations? Demanding sessions between and among human beings are rife with emotion. If you remember back to Chapter 2, it is physiologically true that every thought (a chemical synapse) is accompanied by a chemical signal to the body that we experience as an emotion. It is the stronger emotions that become part of the influence in negotiations.

To build on this, check in with your own personal experience. The more challenging a circumstance or factor is in your life, the more emotion accompanies it. Everyone has these challenges. Work challenges are perhaps the greatest source of emotion even though most of us are asked to manage them so strongly that we can lose sight of the fact they are running behind the scenes. Emotions running behind the scene in negotiations spell danger.

Because it is clear that emotions are present in sessions, why not use that knowledge for the greater good, as an advantage really. Recall times in your own life when things got tough. At work, perhaps you did not get a raise or promotion, or you found working with a particular individual exceedingly difficult. At home you may have anything from a furnace breaking down to your marriage breaking down. Things can get hugely tough as in the loss of a job or the passing of a loved one; small events include such things as being delayed in traffic or paying money for what turns out to be a lousy movie. Our days are constantly filled with challenges.

Each of these difficulties is also an opportunity for empathy. What has it "felt" like for you when you have had a difficult event, let us say you got passed over for a promotion, and someone you respected let you know that they understood and felt your pain. Did that help or hinder? Most humans will say that it helped. You see, empathy bonds. Humans need connection, especially in tough situations (all to varying degrees—remember Behavior Styles). High Doers are more independent and do not want or need soft-sounding (to them) emotional words. High Thinkers are fact-based and less emotion based and so can appreciate harder, detail-oriented relating (empathizing). High Talkers are more apt to want to talk about the pain points and so asking them questions will have them see you as an ally. High Guardians are the most earthy and will most appreciate your warm tones and heartfelt words. There are many shades of gray among the four quadrants.

Here is a caution. Until you get better at purifying your empathy, you may be prone to starting with or adding a "fix" to the interaction. Solving a problem is fine, but empathy is what opens people's receptivity to these solutions. Empathize first, solve the problem second is the key. Practice empathy on its own until you have it down and then add "fixing" suggestions when you are a master empathizer.

Let us use the real estate parties to demonstrate how exchanges might go. The opportunity to empathize could happen anytime you are together. But let us use a simple example that might actually present itself at the very get-go.

SP as Doer: Sorry I'm late. Traffic was really bad.
You: That sounds tough. No problem!

Debrief: Keep it short and not too sweet with Doers. Something like traffic? Hey, it is just a piece of business to deal with. Let us move on to bargaining!

SP as Thinker: Sorry I'm late. Traffic was really bad. I always allow myself 10 extra minutes when I am traveling to a meeting. But there was an accident between an SUV and a pick-up truck at the 401 onramp and after untangling from the backup, I had to take High Street to Route 16 and make my way over here with six traffic lights on the way.

You: That sounds really messy. It's clear that you are very thoughtful of others in leaving home 10 minutes earlier than you think you need. But who can tell when an accident will blow up your planning. It was smart of you to take the route you did as it is the most direct way here given the circumstances. I'm glad you arrived safely.

Debrief: Thinkers = details. They are fact neighbors to Doers but with lots more analysis and detail. So go into detail. And acknowledge the details of their challenge. Although they are more considerate of others than Doers, they still are more cerebral and less touchy feely. So keep your empathizing more to the facts. They will then move on in the session with a bit more trust in you.

SP as Talker: I am sorry I'm late. What a hell of a mess. First I spilled coffee on my shirt and had to change that. Then I ran over my son's skateboard in the driveway and had to give him heck. I couldn't find my usual radio station and missed the exit as I was searching the channels. Then, just as I was about three blocks from here, my cell phone went off. You know I can't talk and drive in this state and it was my wife so what was I to do. Anyway, it's good to see you even though I feel a bit rushed and stressed out.

You: Man, that sounds like so much to have to deal with. What was the worst part of that?

SP Talker: Yada yada yada yada . . . (two minutes' worth).

Debrief: Talkers talk. So when they get into rough situations, ask them questions. If you show interest with your listening, they will feel like you care (and I hope you do). You may need to "intrude" (see Level II Listening later in this chapter) to manage your negotiating time because once a high Talker gets rolling, they could end up anywhere.

SP as Guardian: I am so sorry I am late.

You: Hi (*name*—Guardians appreciate the personal touch). I'm glad you got here.

SP: I don't like holding anyone up. You must have been worried. I hit a horrible traffic jam.

You: Oh (*name*), that sounds awful for you. I know you have the best intentions and you must have been feeling more and more anxious as the slow minutes passed. Are you okay?

Debrief: High Guardians are big hearted, warmer than most people. Although softer in their expressiveness, they do like to hear that they are "good" in whatever ways you can show them. It really means a lot when you can relate to their troubles. The more you *genuinely* relate, the more loyalty they have for you. This kind of bonding certainly helps in negotiations.

Discovery Skill #3—Powerful Questions

Discovery Phase means just that. And what is an essential tool to have in your exploration kit? Asking powerful questions! During the first three years of my training company, Bold New Directions, in every class in which we cover communication skills, I kept track of what percentage of questions asked were closed- versus open-ended. I did this with about a thousand people and globally. The result was learning that 70 percent of questions asked in our skill-building exercises were closed-ended. That only left a paltry 30 percent for open-ended. So what's wrong with that?

In this skill section, in addition to open- and closed-ended questions, we will also cover Leading, Risk-based, and Benefit-based questions for usefulness in sessions.

Closed-ended: Here is why that ratio does not work well. A closed-ended question invites a very short answer.

You: How long have you been trying to sell this property?

SP: Six months!

You: How many other prospects have you met with?

SP: Nine!

You: Do you think you will come down in price?

SP: Perhaps!

With a closed-ended question, you are likely to get a closed-ended response. The brain does not have to work with most sentences that begin with Are . . . , Will . . . , When . . . , Where . . . , Did . . . , Who. . . . An immediate response, such as yes, no, blue, green, right, wrong, may be all you get. That is not helpful when you are opening up a discussion.

Open-ended: What are more reliable in getting more information are big, open-ended questions. A powerful, open-ended question is designed to get the other party to both think and feel about the answer. This is much more engaging and much more useful to you (and in win-win, ultimately to them, too).

You: This property has been on the market a long time. What do you think is going on about that?

You: What have other prospects you've shown this to thought about the opportunity?

You: What will it take for you to come down in price?

You: Tell me more about your reasons for selling.

You: Help me to understand why you don't think you will paint the interior to help seal the deal?

If you craft the sentence well, those that begin with What . . . , How . . . , Tell me more . . . , Help me to understand . . . are more likely to produce more detailed responses. *Note* #1: Sentences like "Tell me more about . . ." and "Help me to understand . . ." are not grammatically questions but rather, requests. But they act in the same way, with the intention of producing more information (to be used on behalf of win-win results).

You can only do your best in inviting people to reveal more information. Negotiations are a dance of trust and revelation. Open communication sounds good but in real life, who puts all their cards on the table at once? Win-win does not mean giving the farm away but trading it acre by acre. When you ask an open-ended question of a high Doer, you are likely you get very short answers. That is their way: direct and to the point. You will need to discover their W.I.I.F.M. to inspire them to talk longer and with more substance. Ask a closed-ended question of a high Talker and they are likely to run with it even as their running is really a hopping from one subject to another. With these folks, you have to manage the conversation on behalf of everyone's time and effectiveness (again, see "intruding" in the upcoming information on Level II Listening).

Here is a last note about the open-ended questions and requests: "Why . . . " and "Explain. . . . " If you use either of these two words to start a sentence, consciously expand your EQ radar for their impact on the other. If you are like many of us, you were grilled as a child and teenager with accusatory questions starting with "Why": "Why were you late last night, young man?" "Why did you eat those cookies when I told you not to?" "Why aren't your grades higher?" This kind of Why does not come from a state of curiosity but rather from the egoic right/wrong mind attempting to hang the victim. Tone of voice is important, too. Remember that we spoke of this in Chapter 7, "Presenting Your Case." Is yours full of interest and situationally appropriate warmth? Or perhaps monotone? Monotone may be interpreted as cold, and who wants to answer a cold question? If you use Why, do your best to sound neutral, as in "Why do you think the market is so tight in this neighborhood?" If you notice any kind of negative reaction (using social awareness) from the other, switch to "what" and "how" questions. The same with beginning a request with "Explain." Many a child has been confronted with "You will *explain* to me what you were doing or else," and rarely in carefree circumstances. So why go there when there are more positive ways of inviting out useful information.

Leading questions: The intent of using leading questions is just that—to lead the other down a path of *your* choosing.

SP: You like this property, right?! (It is a question with a specific answer in mind, right?!)

You: You're going to work exclusively with me on the property, okay?!

These call on the same dynamic as closed-ended questions in that they attempt to stimulate the other's brain to only come up with one answer. And the answer is in *your* favor. What are the ethics involved here in a mutuality-based philosophy? This is where your EQ comes in handy again. Negotiations, including win-win, are a series of give and take. Because the other parties may not be educated/practiced in the overall and long-term effectiveness of mutuality, they may not want to balance the give and take accounting sheet. As you do your best for both of you to come out with good-enough results, leading questions might help you influence some positive responses for your own gain. If nothing else, they test the waters of the other's thinking. If they answer in the affirmative, good for you. If there is pushback, you have an opportunity to explore the "no" using an inviting open-ended question. It is a process.

Risk-based questions: Your job as an asker of questions is to support the process of each party thinking and feeling through as completely as possible. Negotiations that occur haphazardly or incompletely are simply less satisfying. A risk-based question is one that attempts to shed light on negative consequences that may occur if something different is not done.

You: What will it be like for you if you don't sell this property in the next three months?

SP: What kinds of problems will it cause for you if we don't come to agreement on this spectacular deal? (A little leading thrown in.)

We simply do not all think of everything, and cooperative negotiating benefits from each party helping to reveal blind spots in the other. You could even make this dynamic part of the original ground rules, particularly in long, more complex negotiations.

Benefit-based questions: You can also use the opposite approach to risk-based questions. Again, we all have blind spots; as intelligent as you are, we all have deficits in our thought process. You can help each other out. You can ask benefit-based questions to invite the other to consider what positive outcomes arc possible if they take certain actions.

SP: Can you imagine how you will feel right after signing the sales agreement?

You: Can you imagine how you will feel as you sign the sales agreement with me?

When you have a sense through discovery of what the others want in the end (probably many subpoints), you can paint and reinforce a picture of success for them through benefit-based questions.

Questions summary: The five forms of questions covered each have value. When used with emotional intelligence, and incorporating what you learn as you go, they are a most powerful ally. They aid in uncovering valuable information and/or stimulating thoughts and feelings that can lead to positive strategies.

Discovery Skill #4—Requests

How many times have you *not* asked for what you want in life? Why did you not ask? The most frequent reply when I have asked this around the globe is "fear of rejection." This makes sense. Robert Fulghum says that by the time we are four years of age, we have heard the word *no* about 10,000 times. That is a tremendous amount of negative reinforcement. And what is the likelihood in life (and every conversation is a negotiation) of your getting what you want just handed to you if you do not ask for it (a request)? Unlikely! In negotiations, it is crucial to ask for what you want and need.

The following exercise is designed to take the risk out of asking. If you understand that there are really only four basic responses to a request, that is helpful. Two of the four answers already lean to the positive. There are two additional responses that I shed light on to increase the likelihood of positive outcomes. The four responses to a request are:

1. Yes.
2. No.
3. Counterproposal: "I suggest this instead. . . ."
4. Delay: "I need time to think about it."

We go through these one by one using the real estate example.

1. Yes.

You: Will you paint the two rooms I've requested as part of the deal?
SP: Yes!

Those are the easiest.
2. No.

You: Will you paint the two rooms I've requested as part of the deal?

SP: No!

What do you do in response to a no!? As I have facilitated this exercise in classrooms around the world, at least 50 percent of participants, when hearing the word *no*, sit there in silence. Their reinforced neuron/dendrite programming is all too familiar with this negative reply. They passively accept the no! But they also do not get what they asked for (at least from that person).

Einstein suggests that you do not keep on doing what you have always done. Because you will keep on getting what you have always got. What to do? Probe! Get curious about the no! Ask questions to see what is behind the no or to get past that answer as the other's initial or even default response. Let us expand on the example:

You: Will you paint the two rooms I've requested as part of the deal?

SP: No!

You: Mmmm, please tell me more about your reluctance.

SP: Well, I just think that you should take care of that.

You: Thanks. But if you paint those rooms, I would be more inclined to purchase the property, and sooner. I've heard that you use a local painter that you trust (lower cost as this professional is already in place).

SP: I hadn't thought of him. I could consider that. If I arrange for his service, how about we split the cost of the paint?

You: That sounds fair. Let's put it into the agreement.

Debrief: The first key is to not attack the *no* with accusation or blame in your voice or words but to truly be in a state of curiosity. Your warmer tones will tell them you are curious, and their ego will be stimulated to defend their initial negative position. You want to inspire receptivity to getting past the no and at least start a conversation about possibilities. As always, I say that nothing is 100 percent effective in life. But try this probing technique and you will certainly get a higher percentage of plausible options than if you just retreat after your request is rejected.

3. Counterproposal: "I suggest this instead . . ."

This is a good sign and you have now begun a mini-negotiation. New ideas are brought to the table and good-enough solutions can emerge.

You: Will you paint the two rooms I've requested as part of the deal?

SP: Well, I don't want to get directly involved with that. But how about if I give you the name of an expert painter I've used on numerous occasions?

You now have a conversation (negotiation) going that may result in something of worth to you.

4. Delay: "I need time to think about it."

Although this might be a stall tactic, an answer is not always readily apparent to everyone. You will rarely hear this reply from a Doer as they make decisions so quickly (more apt to be a curt yes or no!). But Thinkers do need to think about it. And Guardians often need to check in with others for a consensus decision. Talkers are more likely to either impulsively say yes or no, but they may also want to talk it through with you.

The key to this delay, then, is to ask for a time when they will get back to you (not recommended—passive) or better yet, permission for when you can get back to them (proactive and another mini-negotiation).

You: Will you paint the two rooms I've requested as part of the deal?

SP: Mmmm, I will have to think about it.

You: Fair enough. When can I check back in with you about that? (You then negotiate a mutually agreeable check-in time.)

Request Summary

1. Yes (easiest).
2. No (probe from curiosity).
3. Counterproposal: "I suggest this instead . . ." (work with it).
4. Delay: "I need time to think about it" (get closure about check-in timing).

Discovery Skill #5—Listening

There is nothing better for building rapport than deep listening. Each person benefits. You, the listener, gets to consciously take in information that may prove useful. The person being listened to usually experiences an inner (mostly subliminal) satisfaction as being listened to—honored, if you will. Most people also like telling what they know; it is pleasing to their self-esteem.

But in facilitating listening skills exercises in my travels around the world, most people indicate that they have never had a listening class. Amazing! We talked earlier in the book about the challenges to human receptivity (people only hear about 50 percent of what is said, we go away 6 to 10 times a minute). Yet we rely on information in conversations, meetings, and so on, to make decisions, take actions, and more. I trust that you will agree that enhancing one's ability to listen more deeply will help rather than hinder a negotiation.

Although it is easier to coach improved listening when in person, we can cover some useful tips here in written form, too.

I highlight two forms of listening: Level I and Level II (borrowed from Coaches Training Institute).

Level I Listening Have you ever been interrupted? Someone breaks in on the conversation when you are talking? It appears that their idea or solution is better than yours. Why wait to tell you. They do it now, basically disregarding you. How has that felt for you? If you are like most people, the answers could be: "I felt dismissed, bad, disrespected, irritated, left out. . . ." None of these would inspire you to enthusiastically continue. Just the opposite. These are not the kind of feelings that make a conversation (negotiation) easier.

Now, have you ever interrupted someone else? Yes? Oh, you had "good reasons" (subjective) for doing so. But how do the other people feel who are then overridden by you? Use your EQ to get clear about this one.

So Level I listening is when it is all about *you*. In mutuality-based negotiations, that is not good enough. I like the acronym W.A.I.T. (Why Am I Talking?). You will have your turn. EQ again comes in handy. Self-awareness that you are overtalking them, self-management to W.A.I.T. (and this takes increasing your ability to be patient, something you can do with practice), social awareness about how either choice is affecting the other, and understanding that managing the relationship vis-à-vis listening more fully is an important factor in (negotiation) relationships.

Level II Listening What to do instead of interrupting? Listen at Level II! Level II listening is when it is all about *them*. This includes being in a calm and curious state. Putting your attention in laser focus on them—creating an attitude that they are the most important person in the world in these few seconds of conscious, attentive listening. Your full and undivided presence is viscerally "felt" by you and the other. Your solid eye contact and leaning your body in a bit will give them additional clues that you are there for them in those moments. Doing so inspires people to keep on talking (giving you extra information), trust you more deeply, and reciprocating when it is your turn to speak.

On "Intruding": As we have said, when you interrupt someone, you become the center of attention as you step on the other person's flow of ideas or information. The result is usually negative feelings about the interruption. Intruding sounds quite the same when first observed. You are actually still stopping the other from speaking. But, intruding **has a very different intention**. This is used when Talker behavior has taken over (hijacked the conversation) as they go on and on. They also often roam off target. Neither of you really has time for this. So, to bring the conversation back on track for mutual benefit (instead of interrupting just for you), you step in. But you step in with a respectful tone and intent. It might go like this as you have been discussing preferences for real estate closing dates:

SP: Let me tell you about the things you could do if you finish the basement. Yada yada yada yada . . .

You (with a respectful tone): John, thank you for your creativity but for both our time's sake, it would be best to get back to completing the conversation about closing time frames.

Or, another method . . .

SP: Let me tell you about the things you could do if you finish the basement. Yada yada yada yada . . .

You (breaking in): John, we can come back to the basement at some point, but I wonder if you really think you can finish the roof by November 21?

The three easiest ways to get people off a tangent and back on track are: to use respectful tones, say their name and the reason for stopping them, or asking a question on a topic of mutual interest.

Here's a last note on "intruding" regarding conflict. If the other party is going off on a ramble or persisting argumentatively on a topic, interrupting will throw gas on the fire. Intruding is lost on them as their fair sense of anything goes away during anger (revisit Chapter 6).

Which do you think will serve you (and the other) better? Hands down, it is Level II Listening!

Skill #6—Paraphrasing

This is the last skill we cover in this section. What is paraphrasing? Wikipedia defines it as "a restatement of the meaning of a text or passage using other words."

But I have to disagree with this old definition. When I first became a milieu counselor with rookie exposure to paraphrasing, it was taught in a manner similar to that described on Wikipedia: "Summarize back to the person using your own words." With either definition, here is where the danger lies. If you listen actively at Level II and want to let the other know what you heard, that you are in sync, then you have a bit to say. But the source of that information, the other person, communicated that information in a way that *they* understood; "using other words" or "using your own words" creates the need for translation, and that can complicate communication. The updated practice is to summarize back to the person what you think you heard using *their* keywords or keyword phrases, wrapping your own soft language around their original message. Makes sense! The other person then has the opportunity to add to or correct what you reflected back. This adds additional clarity, a key ingredient to any successful session.

When do you paraphrase? Whenever either one of you has covered information that either party thinks is important enough to spend time summarizing to ensure best communication. The egoic mind likes to think that it is smart and that we hear everything that needs to be heard. That part of the mind then can "pooh pooh" paraphrasing as demeaning. You can discuss the use and usefulness of paraphrasing as yet another item included in the early conversation of setting ground rules in Discovery. Do what works!

Discovery Phase Summary

The Discovery Phase is most likely the least used but most important phase in the negotiations. Getting things settled between you before diving into trading makes all the difference. Open communication, trust, and mutually agreed-on expectations are set here. The skills that you can employ to increase communication and therefore effectiveness are distinguishing objective from subjective messages, employing empathy for additional bonding, purposefully using powerful questions, turning request-asking into a useful practice, deepening your ability to listen at Level II, and finding ways to paraphrase for mutual understanding.

Questions to Ponder
- Have you been guilty of diving into trading too fast?
- Overall, what do you see are the advantages to improve Discovery of others?
- What will you do to notice when people are speaking objectively?
- How many times a day are you willing to tune in to conversations to notice all the subjective terms being used around you?
- Will you take five opportunities every day to empathize with people's small and large troubles?
- What will you look for to determine how your empathizing is working?
- Will you ask at least five closed-ended questions a day and notice the average length of response?
- What will it take for you to use five open-ended questions a day and notice the impact they have on others?
- How many requests will you make per day for the next week (I recommend five).
- How do you now handle the "No's!"?

- Do you arrange a check-in time when people tell you they have to think about your request?
- Do you even know if you currently have a habit of interrupting people?
- What will it take to notice yourself when interrupting, then stopping and saying, "I'm sorry; I interrupted you. Please go on"?
- Will you "intrude" with respect when someone has hijacked the conversation? Any conversation?
- Will you paraphrase (at least a little) five times a day for the next week to practice paraphrasing?

Goals for Success

From the answers you get to the questions above, write S.M.A.R.T. goals that will lead to greater Discovery Phase success.

S.M.A.R.T. Goals for Preparing for Your Session

S. pecific

M. easurable

A. ctionable

R. elevant

T. ime Bound

I will _____

13

Checking In Before Moving On

Check-In Phase

This is a short but vital phase. If you have prepared with full due diligence, completed the Discovery Phase well, and you are clear on behaviors, needs, goals, pressures, and concessions, you just use Check In as a test of readiness to Trade.

If you dive into trade with incomplete preparation and discovery or no check-in, you are bound to run into trouble. Misunderstandings and ensuing conflicts grow quickly from that incompleteness. But they are avoidable. We are all fallible. We all have incompleteness. This phase is designed to support your success with an intentional look to see what you have missed. With a *purposeful assumption* that you missed something. That is a powerful admission and focal point (remember, the ego does not like admitting it is not perfect).

There are some simple questions to use to uncover deficits in preparation or discovery of each other's full range of business and personal concerns. These same techniques may reveal that you are good enough to proceed to actually trading concessions. Some big open-ended questions that can help are:

- What have we missed?
- What have we not covered that may come back to bite us?
- What items did we not address that might prove helpful before getting down to the nuts and bolts?
- What did I miss about how you want to be treated that would be helpful for me to know?
- If we fast-forward to imagine our bargaining, what could come up that should actually be talked about now?
- If you had one more thing to add before beginning the hard-core dealing, what would that be?

You can see that any questions along these lines are more likely to elicit thoughts and feelings that, if not revealed, could prove troublesome in the next phase of trading. Make a list of your own. The key is getting in the practice of intentionally stopping for a moment when you think you are ready to charge in.

In the real estate deal, it might sound like this:

You: If we agreed to talk further about the painting issue, might that open the way to settling other pieces?

Or

You: You said earlier that your business partner was having a few issues with the IRS. What else would be important to reveal that might interfere with our deal?

Or

You: If we can settle on a closing date first, would that help determine the financing options?

You will have to make these up based on the specifics of what you negotiate. But the questions are all designed to qualify some item instead of starting from a competitive or attacking position.

If some ruffling comments come up or you notice body language that indicates less than happiness, you go right back to the Discovery Phase (an anticipated strategy that you can actually design into the process during the initial discovery conversation). Something has not been discussed clearly enough. If you try *trading* at this point, you can imagine that a fight is ahead. Do not allow it. Manage the process!

Checking In Before Moving On Summary

This is a fairly straightforward but critical step within the three phases that involve your direct contact with the other party. The intention is to consciously look for any gaps in knowledge or agreement that, if left unattended, may come back to cause arguments in the Trade Phase. It is a proactive approach to bringing greater ease and mutual success in the often tension-filled arena called negotiating.

Questions to Ponder
- Have you ever given thought to using a check-in (every time)?
- What do you think the advantages will be in your negotiating world?
- What has happened in past negotiations because you headed like a bull into trading?
- What variety of check-in questions will you brainstorm for reducing the misunderstandings and disagreements in your session?

Goals for Success

From the answers you get to the questions above, write S.M.A.R.T. goals that will lead to greater success with checking in.

S.M.A.R.T. Goals for Check-In Success

S. pecific

M. easurable

A. ctionable

R. elevant

T. ime Bound

I will _____

14

Trading for Mutual Gain

Trade Phase

Your preparation is accomplished, your informative discussions feel productive, and you have checked in to test the waters of completeness. It is finally time to trade.

Because you have preagreed about where you will start, you begin with the priority item. If you immediately start to disagree, call for a pause. Overtly point out that returning to the pretrading Discovery Phase will bring you both back onto an agreeable track. Because everything on the table is somehow interconnected, you may quickly discover that what you thought would be best to start with would actually be better talked about after some other influential item. It is all good. As long as you understand this dynamic in advance, it will no longer cause the knee-jerk arguments of the past. You simply attend to shifting to rediscussion.

Money is often the starting point but not always. It will be up to your particular negotiations as to what elements are present. Some negotiations do not even include money per se.

Example: Here is a detailed and amazing nonmonetary example from the Vietnam War Paris peace talks.

The leading delegates took a little less than two months just to agree on the shape of the negotiation's conference table. (Taken from: *Foreign Relations*, 1964–1968, Volume VII, Vietnam, September 1968–January 1969. Released by the Office of the Historian.)

On November 26, 1968, President Thieu of South Vietnam finally agreed to dispatch a delegation to Paris, and made a public announcement the following day (235, 236).

The official talks still did not begin. South Vietnam raised a series of procedural issues, the most prominent of which were the particular use of flags and nameplates, the speaking order of the participants, and the physical arrangement of the conference, including most notably the shape of the conference table. On the latter issue, the North Vietnamese and the National Liberation Front (NLF) insisted on a four-sided table to emphasize equality between the parties, while the United States and especially South Vietnam favored a two-sided arrangement that did not obviously give the NLF equal footing with South Vietnam (250, 260, 264). On January 2, 1969, the North Vietnamese relented on their requirement that made flags and nameplates contingent upon the acceptance by the other side of a continuous round table (268, 269). On January 7 President Johnson sent Thieu a strongly worded message to desist from the "continued stalemate on present lines" that was undermining public support within the United States for South Vietnam (276). Thieu continued to refuse to consider such a trade-off from his original position on the shape of the table (277–279). Pressure on Thieu from Washington coupled with the involvement of Soviet diplomats eventually overcame this impasse. On January 13 the Soviet Ambassador in Paris directed his subordinate to propose a resolution: a round table with two smaller rectangular tables at opposite sides; no flags or nameplates; and speaking order arranged by the drawing of lots (280, 281). Both the North Vietnamese and the American delegations agreed to this proposal on January 15, as did both South Vietnam and the NLF the next day (283, 284). On January 18 the first meeting between the four parties, which focused solely on modalities for the substantive talks, was held (286). The Johnson administration left office on January 20, 1969, with the knowledge that peace talks were finally underway.

It took almost two full months to agree on matters such as nameplates and table shapes. Lots of maneuvering for power can go on in a negotiation. But for everyone involved, it also helps to constantly put these maneuverings into greater context. In the case of the Vietnam War, many human beings were killed in the two months of stalemate and argument. While the impacts of your actions may not be as severe, what are the impacts?

Who Offers First

As covered in Chapter 9 on creating range and alternatives, there are two generally used strategies regarding who names what first. We use the real estate example again. (Remember, similar properties in the neighborhood have been selling at $725,000.)

One rule of negotiations is that whoever names price first (and almost any tradable commodity for that matter), loses. Why? Because you give away your starting position. The other side may have been way off in their guess of what your range is. Now they know and can use that information to their advantage.

You might not have created a big *wish* and are afraid of offending the seller. So you offer first and the figure is $715,000.

The sellers are blown away with delight. In their Preparation Phase, they guessed that you would start at $675,000. In their minds, you just gave them $40,000. They can now adjust their response much higher than they originally aspired to.

The second option is to do excellent due diligence and name the starting position first. Why? Remember that your high aspiration (starting point, high or low, depending on if you are the buyer or seller) can lower or raise the other party's aspiration. It can get them rethinking or even scrambling fast.

SP: Even though similar local properties have been selling in the $725,000 range, through my inside resources, I've learned that the city is going to spend $20 million on a beautification project that will greatly increase the value of everything in this neighborhood. So with that in mind, $775,000 is the new asking price for this duplex.

You: (That news blasts your now really lowball starting point right out of the water.)

You need to know your situation well and choose. If your choice proves less effective than you would wish, you have to recover. There is still plenty of time to negotiate with mutuality. And, in the Evaluate Phase, you will take notes for next time, particularly when negotiating with the same party.

If the negotiating price gets you stuck, remember two things: you can always park it until later and talk about other possible concessions to be traded first. This can ease the tension and get some additional things accomplished. Because these concessions also have monetary amounts associated with them (and do openly state the dollars entailed), agreeing on some of these can also help shape agreements later about direct dollar amounts.

Concessions: Remember, you are always negotiating a total package. Negotiations can be full of concessions traded. In the Preparation Phase, you did everything possible to flesh out your usable list of concessions to offer. These resources, skill-sets, and developed systems are all low cost to you (because you already have them in place) but of high value to the other party. But to truly establish how low a cost they are (because they still are a cost to you), it is best to crunch the numbers on every resource, skill-set, or developed system you offer. That way, you have a clear picture of what that value is of what is going out in relation to what concessions you want to come in.

Real Estate Example

The sellers are considering your request to have two rooms in the rental duplex repainted. Because you have a painter you always use reliably (and they do not) and because you have a great rate on paint at the local building supply store (and the buyer does not), they are considering agreeing. But before agreeing, they will do the math: $25 per gallon for paint (oh, did you forget to negotiate quality?) times so many square feet equals $500. The retiree painter (mmmm, did you negotiate expertise?) gets $20 per hour times an estimated 15 hours equals $300. Total = $800. Now they need to discover what the value is to you. "Must haves" versus "Would like to haves." Remember that "must haves" are the "Whys" of your reason for being there. You cannot, will not trade them away. Be prepared to trade away "would like to haves" but always have them prioritized so you have conscious choices about what to offer or not, and to what degree.

Always ask for something in return: Some of you are nicely generous. This is generally a wonderful trait and we can use more of that on the planet, please. But in negotiations, doing so may backfire on you. If you give something to the other party for free, what does that say about the value of that something? "Low cost to you" does not mean cost-free to you. The principle of reciprocity suggests that people return concessions in kind. So when you offer a concession, you might say something like, "I will give this to you and in return, I would like you to give this to me." Usually I suggest that you be as specific as possible. But once in a while I will say, "What can you give me in return?" as a big open-ended question. Sometimes the other surpasses or even far exceeds my expectations. If they do not, you can then get more specific. Each of you needs to be aware of the underlying monetary value of what you are trading to feel like you are coming out of each particular trade with a win-win. Sometimes, you need to trade two items for their one or get two items in return for your one, all depending on values involved.

Concessions come in innumerable forms. If the overall stakes are high, and the concessions are numerous, the total monetary value can be sizable.

It is also wise to look at your track record for your habits on trading concessions.

Doer: If you have high Doer tendencies, you likely do not ever want to give up anything. ("What's mine is mine . . . and what's yours is negotiable.")

Thinker: If you have lots of practiced Thinker traits—in this case we-based—you may approach negotiating as if there is going to be a fair exchange. But Doers do not play fair, and Talkers, if pushed, get highly competitive. So you may give away too many concessions thinking that you will get equal concessions in return. Look back to see how that is working for you.

Talker: Your concession-giving may be erratic. Your impulsiveness may have you giving more away than you need to for something that strikes you of high value in the moment. In retrospect, perhaps your interest was short-lived but you are still stuck with having traded too high for that item. And you may resist giving anything at all if you get too aggressive in competitiveness. Balance will be your key.

Guardians: Like Thinkers, you may also give away too many concessions. But for you, this is usually because you do not like anything conflictual, and trading usually has some tugging to it. But the good news is that you can change habits and so you can become stronger at a more fair game of trading.

Positionality: If you get stuck, always come back to the Why of your being there. This reminds both sides of the essential reasons for negotiating in the first place. It refreshes all the common ground you have uncovered. And, it can effectively let the "stuck" energy dissipate. Remember, too, that there are 18 ways of doing or achieving anything (at least as an attitude). If the strategy you have been using takes you down a dead-end street, get creative. Toss things onto the table of possibility. What do you have to lose?

When two parties get positional and no forward motion is occurring (stalemate), take a break. Our brains get tunnel vision and need some fresh air for a fresh mind.

Tactics might also emerge in this phase if they have not before. The topic of tactics is so important that I have devoted the entire next section to it. Tactics can totally throw a negotiation off track. So study the next section well and then reexamine the Trade Phase with your newfound ability to expose and eliminate tactics in mind.

One last reminder about Why you are there. All the exceptional price and concessions-trading is worthless unless what you trade meets your mutual Why goals. They are always at the heart and center of every single negotiation you will ever be involved in.

Trading for Mutual Gain Summary

Trading is the fourth phase of negotiating. When you master the skills of preparing, discovering, and checking-in, trading becomes so much easier, with greatly reduced disagreement. Know your prioritized list of concessions to trade. Know the monetary value of each item. Never give without getting. Get creative, especially when either of you gets positional or stuck.

Questions to Ponder
- What is in it for you (W.I.I.F.M.) to spend lots more time in Phases I, II and III?
- What do you need to do to change your habit of trading too quickly before completing the three prior phases?
- What has been your concession-trading pattern? (Give away too much? Give away too little? Give things away for free?)
- How will you use the dissolving conflict strategies when trading gets hard and argumentative?

Goals for Success

From the answers you get to the questions above, write S.M.A.R.T. goals that will lead to greater success when trading.

S.M.A.R.T. Goals for Trading Success
S. pecific
M. easurable
A. ctionable
R. elevant
T. ime Bound
I will _____

15

Evaluating for Improvement

Evaluate Phase

We said at the start that many, many negotiators use only two phases, Prepare and Trade. Those who do not *evaluate* do not learn. And every single conscious negotiation has learning opportunities for the next negotiation. Over time, your negotiating success will certainly improve if you evaluate your efforts.

So, evaluate how you did as soon as possible after each session, every session, even if the entire negotiation is not complete.

Areas to Consider

List and celebrate your successes: This is a practice that applies to building on the positive. Our confidence and self-esteem build when we openly (to ourselves, at least) acknowledge things we did well along with the benefit-laden results we have achieved. The science of epigenetics tells us that sending our DNA signals of success causes them to express more positively. We feel better. That certainly helps everything.

Do what better and how? Break down every possible aspect of the negotiation. What phases did you excel at? Which phases could you improve? Within each phase, look for subpoints that could use some tweaking next time.

What other approaches next time? Remember that attitudinally, there are 18 ways to do anything. Our brains like using established mental pathways. But that just has us doing what we have always done. The key to mastery is changing for what works better.

How did you handle emotion? Because our biological-chemical make-up is that every thought (a chemical synapse) produces a chemical message to the body that we call an emotion, this area may have lots of opportunity for you. Reread Chapters 3 and 6 on expanding emotional intelligence and dissolving conflict. This is an area in which humans (you!) can constantly improve for life.

How can you improve your team play? What did you observe that worked and did not work with your teammates? What do you need to do to work more compatibly with behavioral styles that are not your natural allies? How can you use EQ's social awareness of them and managing your relationships with them? What can you do in the Preparation Phase to create a stronger code of conduct and practical ground rules? How can each team player's role be even more clearly defined?

What did you forget to do? The list of things to do in a complex or lengthy negotiation can be quite long. What memory aids do you employ? What written reminders do you use? How can you make your negotiation to-do list more complete?

How can your preparation serve more fully? Although time is always a factor, what can you do next time in the Preparation Phase that will help in both Discovery and Trading phases?

If you are in a team negotiation, do this evaluation by yourself and also with the entire group. Some group members may say they do not have time for this. Remind them of Einstein's definition of insanity: *doing the same things over and over again and expecting different results*. Another way of saying this is, "If you keep on doing what you've always done, you will keep on getting what you've always got." Develop an attitude that what you do can always be improved.

Evaluating for Improvement Summary

When you are thorough in using the Prepare, Discovery, Check In, Trade, and Evaluate phases, you are doing everything possible to promote strong and mutuality-based negotiations. In today's ever-increasing "do more with less" time crunch, evaluating may go out the window. But if you are reading this book, you will most likely be in many, many negotiations before your days are through. So think of the long-term benefits that putting in short-term evaluation time will bring you. That is what is in it for you to do it!

Questions to Ponder
- If you are not evaluating now after each negotiation, why would it serve you to begin the practice?
- If you are in the habit of evaluating after each and every session, how can you improve your process?
- Even if you are not negotiating as part of a team, how can you pass along your evaluation discoveries to others in your organization who might benefit from your findings?
- What can you do to encourage your colleagues to evaluate and to share their findings with you?
- What can you do to reward yourself for positive reinforcement when you uncover successes in your negotiating process?

Goals for Success

From the answers you get to the questions above, write S.M.A.R.T. goals that will lead to greater evaluation success.

S.M.A.R.T. Goals for Evaluation Success

S. pecific

M. easurable

A. ctionable

R. elevant

T. ime Bound

I will _____

16

Disposing of Tactics

Exposing Tactics

What is a tactic? For the sake of this book, this learning, I ask that you work with the more negative meaning rather than as a synonym for *strategy*. Here it is used for negative leverage, a "negotiator's ability to make his opponent suffer." Words like ambushes, seeking and turning flanks, and creating and using obstacles and defenses are associated. These are all designed to put you into a negative emotion, a state of vulnerability, and to get something from you without giving in return. This definition comes from the military, where the attempt is to get the "enemy" from behind a protected position into the open—a vulnerable open. Then, strike. None of that is conducive to mutuality-based negotiating.

With this definition, then, we consider tactics a negative process. I am taking a bit of space in this book to address some of the more common tactics, not to teach you how to use them but to bring awareness that they might be used against you. After that, your own moral compass needs to guide you.

The Use of Tactics

There are a huge range of tactics to consider that may be used *against* you in your negotiations. Over the next few pages we examine a representative set of tactics, clarify with examples, and discuss strategies to probe and dispose of the tactic. Though you can find many more on the web, I trust that by the end of this chapter, you will be clear about what process to use in dealing with tactics used against you.

Your primary challenge about tactics is this: Is what you are observing a tactic or not? As defined here, a tactic is an *intentional* or *deliberate* attempt to put you in a weakened position. The other party has a strategy when using a tactic. When this particular action is used, the other is engaged in win-lose negotiating—they win and you lose.

But sometimes what you are observing is simply a reality and not an attempt to get you to give without receiving in return. Your job is to determine which is true. One is innocent and one is not. The following tactic examples will help you to discover which is a deception and which is reality.

Better Offer

Let us run through this first tactic together to better understand what the tactic is and how to deal with it.

Description When you make an offer, the sellers say that they have already received a better offer from somebody else.

Example Someone has already made a better offer on this property.

Probe to Expose Is it a tactic or is it real?

This is a tactic if they did not in fact have a better offer made to them. They would be trying to get you to improve your offer or to at least influence your Range and Alternatives.

If you have done your homework in the Preparation Phase, you will clearly have your Range and Alternatives, Bottom Line, BATNA and WATNA in place. So you know where you are willing to go and where you are not willing to go.

Ask what the other offer is. They may or may not choose to tell you. Also explore whether this offer in its entirety (not just price) is "apples to apples." Do not assume that all the content in the offer is the same as what you have been discussing with them.

This is *not* a traditional tactic if they in fact did receive a better offer. Their naming this other offer is simply good negotiating, using competition as leverage to get you to improve your offer.

Better Than That

Let us run through this next tactic together to better understand what the tactic is and how to deal with it.

Description   When you make an offer, the sellers say, "You'll have to do better than that!"

They might accompany this with a saddened, shocked, or disgusted look. Then they may be quiet and wait for you to increase your offer.

Example   Oh, come on. I know you've studied local property market conditions. You'll have to do better than that.

Probe to Expose   Is it a tactic or is it real?

This is a tactic if it is designed to pressure you into a knee-jerk response of quickly making a better offer.

Ask questions like, "What do you mean by better?" Or, "What do you think a fairer offer would look like?"

Also remind them of the other aspects of the deal that will be of benefit to them. Have them once again look at the entire picture and not just the price.

This is *not* a tactic if they had a very different offer in mind and you actually took them by surprise.

Bluff

Let us run through this next tactic together to better understand what the tactic is and how to deal with it.

Description　The other person may confidently tell you something not true to try to impress you in order to get what they want.

Example　I've already received three solid offers on this duplex this week.

Probe to Expose　Is it a tactic or is it real?

This is a tactic, plain and simple. Bluffing is lying. One way to treat all negotiations is to not "believe" anything. By "believe" I mean taking at face value anything and everything that is said (or in some cases, even shown). At the heart of all negotiations should be "Objective Criteria." Simply stated, this is verifiable information—proof.

Be aware that not everyone lives honestly or for mutuality. It is certainly easier to fully trust when you know someone well and have negotiated with them a number of times. Relationships and trust do take time to grow.

If you discover that the sellers are lying, let them know how this will jeopardize your relationship. Lead them back to the concept of mutuality and the value of having a long-term negotiating relationship. They may be sabotaging a very good deal with you.

The bottom line is that it is always up to you to take responsibility to do the best due diligence possible. In negotiations, asking for Objective Criteria is the surest way to stay on a truthful track.

Breaking It Off

Let us run through this next tactic together to better understand what the tactic is and how to deal with it.

Description The other threatens to break off the negotiation.

They can also threaten to break off relationships. When they have a relationship with you, this can be particularly effective for getting you to come back to the fold.

Example I'm sorry. If you will not increase your bid for this duplex, then I can't continue.

Probe to Expose Is it a tactic or is it real?

This is a pressure tactic if done deliberately to get you to make a stronger offer.

First, ask them to stay. Remain friendly. If meeting in person, stand up, move your geographical location even to just the other side of the room. Create a break and a new approach.

Second, get wonderfully curious and be prepared to empathize with their possible frustration. Ask for a clear explanation of why they feel like leaving. If there is truth, then discover it. If this is a tactic, there will not be much substance for them to reveal. Get back to the "Why" of the negotiation.

This is not a tactic when they are simply tired of the process and they think you have not been moving quickly or fairly enough.

Switch Negotiators

Let us run through this next tactic together to better understand what the tactic is and how to deal with it.

Description The sellers change the person who is doing the negotiation for their side. They explain that the previous negotiator has been called away. The new negotiator then goes over all the decisions and agreements with a fine-toothed comb, weeding out all the exchanges that he or she does not like. In fact, the new negotiator may try to start the process from scratch.

Example   John (the property owner) had to attend to business elsewhere. He asked me to take over.

Probe to Expose   Is it a tactic or is it real?

This is a tactic if a new negotiator is artificially inserted into the process, when in fact the first negotiator could still viably be the negotiator. But, less ethical organizations that practice negotiating "at" instead of negotiating "with" may change the negotiator to shake things up if the negotiation is not going their way. Or, they may change negotiators simply to throw you off guard.

As always, inquire. Whether this is a tactic or not, keep great written records as you go through all phases of a negotiation. If they switch players, you do not have to start afresh but continue more seamlessly from where you last ended.

If it is a tactic, speak plainly with the other party about your desire to do business with them repeatedly over time but only if they honor the value of honesty that you agreed upon in the Discovery Phase.

This is not a tactic if something has truly happened to the original negotiator. This could involve personal circumstances like getting sick. There could be professional situations where they get reassigned or their specific skills are more urgently needed on another project.

Agenda Control

Let us run through this next tactic together to better understand what the tactic is and how to deal with it.

Description   If you are not co-agreeing on the agenda and its prioritization, the other party can try to control what is being discussed by deciding what will and will not be on the agenda. The other party can also control the meeting while it is running, particularly if they are chairing it, by encouraging talk about an item or closing it down quickly.

Example   Since this is my property, I think it only right that we follow the list of items I put forth. I know the duplex much better than you. (Also employs the Influence principle of "Authority.")

Probe to Expose   Is it a tactic or is it real?

This is a tactic if the other party intends to run you over in the negotiations process instead of being collaborative. This is clearly a win-lose attitude.

During your Preparation Phase, you need to make clear what you want on the agenda, get agreement for inclusion, and in what initial order you propose attending to the items.

But in mutuality-based negotiations, you are not alone or controlling. This is a co-created process. In the Discovery Phase, talk clearly about your agenda and openly invite the other party to clearly state theirs. Then, agree on a starting point and make sure that each party understands why you all are starting there.

Make sure you have assigned a gatekeeper (yourself if negotiating alone) to stop proceedings if you have wandered too far from the agreed agenda. You check in and see if continuing off that agenda is appropriate or not. One thing always leads to another and you can go astray if not consciously monitoring the direction of the negotiations.

This is not strictly a tactic if the other party's personality is a dominant one. Years of living this way is not a tactic but a way of life. You will have to be stronger and use your EQ and knowledge of behavior styles to better understand how they view the world.

Deadline

Let us run through this next tactic together to better understand what the tactic is and how to deal with it.

Description   The other party sets a deadline by which time you have to decide or act. They make it clear this is an absolute deadline that must be met.

As the deadline approaches, they increase the emotional atmosphere, talking more about what will happen if the deadline is missed. This may be specific (with threatening actions) or vague (with disturbing hints). Often, they cite factors that seemingly cannot be challenged, such as contract completion dates or demands made by others in authority.

Example   I must have your answer about the duplex before we leave today. I am talking to my business partner Tom later and he needs to know the outcome.

Probe to Expose   Is it a tactic or is it real?

This is a tactic if they are consciously putting undue pressure on you simply to get you to move in the direction they want. This does not include finding a collaborative timeline with you. You must first find out if the deadline is "real" or made up as a pressure tactic. By "real" I mean, does this deadline have origins outside of the current negotiations? Are there time agreements with other vendors, customers, and so on that are carried forward into this negotiation? Ask! And even if the answer is yes, is this negotiation really bound by this deadline? People make deadlines; however, for the right reasons, people can also reschedule deadlines. Make your case as mutually beneficial as possible (W.I.I.F.T.—What's In It For Them to move the deadline).

As with all tactics, if the deadline proves arbitrary or contrived, exposing that will have the tactic lose its power.

This is *not* a tactic if there truly are outer-imposed timelines.

Delays

Let us run through this next tactic together to better understand what the tactic is and how to deal with it.

Description Some negotiators will intentionally use time to stretch out the negotiation, especially at critical moments.

Example   I know I said I could meet for an hour but something has come up that I have to attend to.

Probe to Expose   Is it a tactic or is it real?

This is a tactic when the other party fabricates a need to slow down the process.

When you notice that what seems an unusual amount of time is being asked for or taken, diplomatically inquire about what is going on. If you have encouraged openness and mutuality from the start, it is less likely that tactics such as delays will occur. Opening a conversation on the subject is the first step in exposing a tactic if indeed it is one.

This is not a tactic if it is not intentional. They might simply have to go to the bathroom. They may truly feel ill and need to take an overnight break. Some people's behavior style (Thinkers and Guardians) is to be very cautious and they need lots of time and space in process and decision making.

As always, become curious from a place of service to the negotiation. If someone is having a hard time making a decision, see where they are stuck and why. If you are an ally, instead of an enemy, most things can be worked out.

Catastrophizing

Let us run through this next tactic together to better understand what the tactic is and how to deal with it.

Description   Some parties will paint an overly black picture. They describe the outcome of any suggestion in negative terms. They appear pessimistic and gloomy.

They describe only the things they do *not* want in this negative way.

In contrast, they will describe what they do want in a positive light, hoping to have you feel relief from the darker points and say yes to their preferences. (Influence's dynamic of "Contrast.")

Example   This property is a great investment now but if you wait, the market will probably go up, leaving you out in the cold.

Probe to Expose   Is it a tactic or is it real?

This is a tactic if a gloomy picture is painted with a direct attempt to get you in a vulnerable position. To test if this is a tactic, always return to objective criteria instead of emotional appeal. What is, is. The pessimism could be a spin. Weed out the negative subjective additions.

This is *not* a tactic if this is how they view life. There are pessimists in the world who see most of life as a glass half empty. Empathize with them but do not agree. You be the leader. You take the higher, positive road.

Empty Wallet

Let us run through this next tactic together to better understand what the tactic is and how to deal with it.

Description   After you make a request, the other party says that they cannot afford it, have not got it, cannot do it, or otherwise are unable to give you what you want.

Example   I'm sorry, there's just not enough room in the deal to throw in that room painting you want done.

Probe to Expose   Is it a tactic or is it real?

This is a tactic when they do have the resources but want you to back down from a request. As always, you need to probe. Who set the budget? Who has authority to make exceptions?

This is *not* a tactic when there truly is only so much and that is all there is. Get creative. Look at the entire spectrum of possible concessions. What can be substituted? What can be traded later? Where can quality be reassessed for more affordable value?

Façade

Let us run through this next tactic together to better understand what the tactic is and how to deal with it.

Description They may dress well and pretend to be affluent. Or dress down and pretend to be poor. They may mention qualifications that they do not have. Talk about experiences that they have not had. Name-drop about people they have not met. Mention their membership in exclusive clubs. Or otherwise pretend to be someone they are not. Their hope is that if you consider them more important, you may concede things to their higher power. (Again, influence's "Authority," and high Talkers and Guardians are particularly susceptible to this.)

Example When I was giving a keynote at the Landlord's Association . . .

Probe to Expose Is it a tactic or is it real?

This is a tactic if people make things up to impress and sway you. The key is to look for proof through objective criteria. And let the other party know how being disingenuous tarnishes reputations and relationships.

This is *not* a tactic when you are dealing with someone who has a large ego. This may be someone who does not feel his or her natural goodness and so craves recognition from others. In this case, you might ask your own ego to step aside and give special recognition to the needy party.

False Praise

Let us run through this next tactic together to better understand what the tactic is and how to deal with it.

Description The other person tries to make you look good with no particular cause. They tell you how clever, intelligent, attractive, and so on you are. (Talkers can eat this up without questioning.)

Example I never met a real estate prospect like you who did so much research beforehand.

Probe to Expose Is it a tactic or is it real?

This is a tactic if it is disingenuous. Thank the person for their noticing that about you but then get back to business. If it keeps up, ask them directly why they are being so gushingly praise-filled. Acknowledge whatever they say and ask them to focus on objective criteria.

This is *not* a tactic when someone is of a certain kind of social behavior style. Someone who perhaps needs the flattery themselves will also give more flattery. In this case, just accept that flattery is part of their style and experience a little emotional discomfort for the sake of the negotiation.

Forced Choice

Let us run through this next tactic together to better understand what the tactic is and how to deal with it.

Description When offering a set of options, they attempt to make it easy for you to choose the one they want you to choose and hard for you to choose the ones they do not want you to choose.

Methods they can use for this include:

- Offer the thing they want you to take first or last.
- Make the thing they want you to take more memorable (and other things less memorable).
- Make the thing they want you to choose seem more desirable (Influence's "Scarcity").
- Create *contrast* to highlight and polarize the desirable and undesirable.
- Offer things that may normally be acceptable but that they know are unacceptable to you (leaving the obvious choice the one they prefer).

Example Do you want me to have the two rooms painted or the sidewalk repaired?

Probe to Expose Is it a tactic or is it real?

This is a tactic when there are obviously more choices than they are declaring. Your due diligence in the Preparation Phase will help immensely. Question, question, question!

This is *not* a tactic when there are only the offered choices.

Splitting

Let us run through this next tactic together to better understand what the tactic is and how to deal with it.

Description They break everything down into small packages and then negotiate them one at a time. If they are selling things, they price them individually as if in a vacuum.

They may focus first on selling or negotiating the main item. Then show that extra pieces are needed. They will avoid talking about the total cost until you have agreed on each item individually.

Example   We built the garage later and then added the utility shed. We will have to discuss them separately.

Probe to Expose   Is it a tactic or is it real?

This is a tactic if they purposefully want to make the negotiations more complex and confuse you into paying more for the total package than if you agreed to an all-inclusive price.

Although this may be their standard way of doing business, you can lead the way to a more mutually beneficial process and outcome. Use the Preparation Phase to detail every item and every projected cost possible. Then in the Discovery Phase, get all the items on the table that will be addressed in the Trade Phase. This way, you create the big picture of where you are going and will not be as susceptible to the segmented approach.

This is *not* a tactic if they have a demonstrable policy and procedure guiding this methodology.

Good Guy/Bad Guy (Also Known as Good Cop/Bad Cop)

Let us run through this next tactic together to better understand what the tactic is and how to deal with it.

Description   One person acts in an aggressive and pushy way, making unreasonable demands and requiring compliance.

The other person then acts in a kind and friendly way, requesting and getting compliance.

The good guy (or woman) may apologize for the bad guy, or make a case for agreement because the bad guy is being horrible to the good guy, too.

They can even do this as one person: be unpleasant and then apologize and ask nicely for what they want.

Example   SP #1: You will have to paint those rooms on your own. I'm not here to run a charity, you know!

SP Partner (in a much more peaceful tone of voice): Don't mind Tom; he's just having a bad day. If we paint the two rooms for you, what will you give us in return?

Probe to Expose   Is it a tactic or is it real?

This is a tactic if it is done intentionally to set you up emotionally to react favorably to the good guy's offer. It is pretty easy to spot. If someone is coming on aggressively or combatively, watch your emotions. Stay cool. Look to see if the good guy/woman comes in. Looking for the contrast will make it obvious.

The bottom line will always be to return to "Why" you are there. Again, using objective criteria is the key instead of being swayed emotionally. Your Preparation Phase will serve you well if this occurs.

This is *not* a tactic if the other party works as a team and one of them is simply a miserable human being. If alone, they have a dual personality. Forgive them and be glad that you do not live like that.

Legal

Let us run through this next tactic together to better understand what the tactic is and how to deal with it.

Description   They may act like a lawyer, cross-examining the witness (you) and postulating probabilities. They use logical *arguments* that are rational and have past precedence.

They follow the law (Policies & Procedures, rules . . .) to the nth degree.

Example   The town regulations say that I cannot build a garbage containment unit you want within 15 feet of the dwelling.

Probe to Expose   Is it a tactic or is it real?

This is a tactic if they use skewed or even false "objective" criteria. You must continue using your due diligence to research if the documentation is accurate and, more importantly, if it is relevant to your current negotiation. Do not take it on face value. Make sure you negotiate enough time to verify the information.

This is *not* a tactic if they are doing what good negotiators do, which is to use convincing and true objective criteria to make their point.

Nibbling

Let us run through this next tactic together to better understand what the tactic is and how to deal with it.

Description   The other party asks for small things, one at a time, and often at the end. They look to get agreement on each. They portray the request as being very easy for you to give. They will be appreciative when you give and reward you with kind words and thanks (not reciprocal concessions).

They might leave a gap between each item. They can go for a short sequence of nibbles and then give it a rest before asking for more. This can be particularly effective near the end of the negotiation, when you think that you are pretty much done and are seeking to reach a final agreement. You might knee-jerk a "Yes" just to move on.

Example   Oh, I almost forgot. The tenant in unit two has snuck in a cat. You can deal with that, can't you? (Nonmonetary but still a concession involving your time and emotion.)

Probe to Expose   Is it a tactic or is it real?

This is a tactic if they intentionally want to get things of small value from you without giving anything in return.

The rule of negotiating is "never give without getting." That does not mean that in every small instance, you trade of equal quantity and value. What it does mean is that you keep mutuality and reciprocity in mind over the length of the negotiation. You may give back right away or it may come bundled as something additional a little later on.

This is *not* a tactic if the person has been trained this way and does not know the damage it can cause. It is your job to teach them and lead the way to enlightened, mutuality-based negotiating.

No Authority

Let us run through this next tactic together to better understand what the tactic is and how to deal with it.

Description   They refuse to give in on items based on the fact that they have not been given authority to do what is being requested by you.

They might offer to take the request back to that authority for consideration (and, at the next meeting, tell you that the request has been turned down).

Example   I am sorry, but my partner makes all of those decisions about our properties.

Probe to Expose   Is it a tactic or is it real?

This is a tactic if the party you are dealing with does indeed have the authority to make the deal. This can be a delay tactic. It is also intended to get you thinking to yourself, negotiating with yourself. And we usually negotiate ourselves down.

To avoid this in the future, always find out before the negotiating begins if the other party has the authority to trade. If not, find out who has the authority. Diplomatically determine whether it would be best to deal directly with the person who has the authority.

This is *not* a tactic if the other party's organization has an official multilayered or stratified negotiating process. Still, it is your job to find this out in advance.

Nonnegotiable

Let us run through this next tactic together to better understand what the tactic is and how to deal with it.

Description   They identify one or more items as issues on which they will not concede. They might try and distract you from persisting to probe about these items by offering a concession on something else.

Example   I'm sorry, I can't offer you that option.

Probe to Expose   Is it a tactic or is it real?
This is a tactic if the item in question is actually negotiable but they are playing hard to get. Playing hard to get is designed to get you to offer more than you were initially willing to, going past your bottom line. As always, probe. Ask why it is non-negotiable. Use a diplomatic phrase like "Help me to understand. . . ."
This is *not* a tactic if the subject is truly nonnegotiable. Remember the "Why," "What," and "How." The Why includes everything that truly is nonnegotiable, personal, and business.

Take It or Leave It

Let us run through this next tactic together to better understand what the tactic is and how to deal with it.

Description   When the other party makes an offer, they say, "take it or leave it."
They may leave a long *pause* after this (as discussed in Chapter 7), just looking at you in silence, waiting for you to cave in.

Example   We've covered anything worth discussing. That's my final offer.

Probe to Expose   Is it a tactic or is it real?

This is a tactic if they truly have no intention of taking it or leaving it but are trying to create pressure or desperation in you.

Probe! Ask questions to see why they are taking this position. Recall all of the good things you have already agreed on. Ask what else is going on for them.

This is *not* a tactic if they are truly at the end of their rope. Remember, different personalities have different tolerances, different speeds of operating. Like you, they also have a bottom line. And sometimes people simply have a bad day. Take a break if necessary; they might recover some negotiating energy.

Either way, the main thing is to get them to sit down again, now or soon.

The Wince

Let us run through this next tactic together to better understand what the tactic is and how to deal with it.

Description   When you name your price or what you want in exchange for what they are offering, they visibly wince. They look startled and shocked. They look at you in silent disbelief. (Remember Dr. Mehrabian's research that about 60 percent of what we believe is from what we take in visually?) And then they wait for you to make another offer.

Example

You: I am willing to pay $670,000 for the duplex.
SP: (Wince.)

Probe to Expose   Is it a tactic or is it real?

This is a tactic if the body language is premeditated or practiced as a standard, nonmutuality-based way of negotiating. Do not fall into their trap. This is not about you, it is about them.

Ask what is going on for them. See what they are objecting to. Ask them to help you to understand what would be preferable.

This is not a tactic if they are truly surprised at your offer. Talk about their surprise with openness and nonjudgment. Learn what they are thinking and feeling.

Also, remember that different personalities express differently. Some people are very expressive physically and emotionally. That is simply their way.

Disposing of Tactics Summary

Mutuality-based negotiators do not use *tactics*. They work *with* the other party, doing their best to support everyone getting as much as possible at the best cost, repeatedly over time. The key to disposing of a tactic used against you is to name it and probe it with curiosity to determine whether it is an intentional "tactic" or a real circumstance.

Questions to Ponder
- Do you use tactics?
- Why have you used tactics (as defined in this book)?
- What alternatives are there to tactics that will still get you what you want?
- Have you challenged people on their use of tactics against you?
- What has been the result of your exposing their negative tactics?
- What strong but nonaccusatory powerful questions can you use to dispose of tactics?
- What additional tactics have been used against you that would be helpful to study against future negative (to you) results?

Goals for Success

From the answers you get to the questions above, write S.M.A.R.T. goals that will lead to greater success in disposing of tactics.

S.M.A.R.T. Goals for Disposing of Tactics

S. pecific

M. easurable

A. ctionable

R. elevant

T. ime Bound

I will _____

17

Practicing for Life

You have come to the end of this book. But you are only beginning the next phase of enlightened, mutuality-based negotiating. Good things are not necessarily easy, and taking your newfound discoveries out into the real world is no exception. The business world can be hard, as can your personal world. But leading the way to more positive, peaceful negotiating with new skills and insights can be a wonderfully fulfilling adventure. You can inspire change in your circles of influence. You can expand the use of the win-win approach. If you are awake in this world, you know that we all need more of that.

I wish you greater fulfillment in your relationships. I wish you ever-increasing success on each and every next negotiation. Go get 'em!

Appendix

Bold New Directions' Negotiation Preparation Worksheet

Your Strengths	Other Party's Strengths

Your Weaknesses	Other Party's Weaknesses

Your Negotiating Style	Other Party's Negotiating Style

	Yours	Other Party's
Wish		
Starting Point		
Bottom Line		
BATNA		
WATNA		
"Why's"		
"How"		

"Whats" (Concessions): Name 10 You Can Give and the Cost to You
_____ $ _____
_____ $ _____
_____ $ _____
_____ $ _____
_____ $ _____
_____ $ _____
_____ $ _____
_____ $ _____
_____ $ _____
_____ $ _____

"Whats" (Concessions): Name 10 You Want to Get and the Cost to the Other Party

_____ $ _____

_____ $ _____

_____ $ _____

_____ $ _____

_____ $ _____

_____ $ _____

_____ $ _____

_____ $ _____

_____ $ _____

_____ $ _____

Common Ground

Opposing Interests

Differing Interests

Anticipated Tactics

Team Member's Expertise and Negotiation's Role

Develop Five Initial Open-Ended Questions to Ask

Resources

- Visit www.negotiationsinstitute.com to get free reports.
- Call us at 1-800-501-1245 to discuss training programs.
- Write to us at info@boldnewdirections.com.
- Sign up for our free monthly newsletter via www.boldnew directions.com.

Index